W9-BER-308

40's & 50's
COLLECTIBLES
FOR FUN & PROFIT

William C. Ketchum, Jr.

HPBooks ®

Publisher: Rick Bailey
Editorial Director: Randy Summerlin
Editor: Jacqueline Sharkey
Art Director: Don Burton
Book Manufacture: Anthony B. Narducci
Typography: Cindy Coatsworth, Michelle Carter

Published by HPBooks, Inc.
P.O. Box 5367
Tucson, AZ 85703
602-888-2150
ISBN: 0-89586-248-4
Library of Congress
  Catalog Card Number: 85-80121
©1985 HPBooks, Inc.
Printed in U.S.A.
1st Printing

Prepared for HPBooks by Sophia Books/Layla Productions, Inc.
Publisher: Carol Paradis
Designer: Allan Mogel

The author would like to thank the following who lent
assistance and permission to make photographs for this book:

Penelope Byham, New York, New York
Elaine Dilof, Greenwich, Connecticut
Osna Fenner, Brooklyn, New York
The Greenwich Auction Room Ltd., New York, New York
Barbara Marcu, Rye Brook, New York
Alan Moss Studios, New York, New York
Speakeasy Antiques, New York, New York
Albert Squillace, New York, New York

All photos by Calabro Studios, except for the following:
Chun Y. Lai—10 top/bottom, 11 top/bottom, 12 top/bottom, 13, 14 top/bottom,
15 top, 17 bottom, 69, 74 top, 75, 76 top/bottom, 77 bottom.
Schecter Lee—9, 23 top/bottom, 24, 25, 26, 27 top/bottom, 33 top, 71 top, 84, 85
Peter Mauss—16, 17 top, 77 top

Notice: The information in this book is true and
complete to the best of our knowledge. All
recommendations are made without guarantees
on the part of the author or HPBooks. The author
and publisher disclaim all liability in connection
with the use of this information.

40's & 50's COLLECTIBLES FOR FUN & PROFIT

William C. Ketchum, Jr.

Getting Started

The 1940s and 1950s were a fascinating era. Today, thousands of Americans collect furniture, plastics, movie memorabilia and clothing from this period. These items are popular because the 1940s and 1950s were the years of the baby boom. Children born during this time are now grown and have families of their own. They look back on their childhoods and recall with nostalgia the things they grew up with. They want to collect these items and share them with their children.

WHY 1940s AND 1950s MEMORABILIA ARE POPULAR

Fortunately, the 1940s and 1950s provided more collectibles than any other era. After World War II ended, American companies began manufacturing consumer goods again. Thousands of factories produced millions of items. Most of these mementos are collectible. Because so many items are available, prices are relatively low. The situation is ideal for the aspiring collector.

HOW THIS BOOK HELPS

This book is designed to make collecting profitable and fun. It contains information every collector wants to know, including where to find mementos and how much to pay for them. This book will help you to:

Identify Memorabilia—This book also provides important information about the history, background and availability of different types of collectibles.

Invest Wisely—Mementos from this era include readily available, inexpensive items and rare, costly pieces. There is something for everyone at every price. The price guide in this book will help you determine how much to pay when you buy a memento, and how much to charge when you sell one. Everybody has heard stories—which unfortunately are often true—about unsuspecting collectors selling valuable pieces for a fraction of their worth.

Tips given in this book about recognizing, dating and evaluating 1940s and 1950s memorabilia will help you avoid such disasters. If you need more information about a specific collectible, turn to the bibliography. It lists the best books about each type of memento.

Meet Other Collectors—As you become more involved in collecting, you might want to join a collectors' club. This book provides hints about meeting other collectors at shows and auctions. Such contacts are invaluable. Collectors can provide you with information and ideas about where to find items that interest you.

Clean, Restore and Display Collectibles—Collecting involves more than just finding things. Your acquisitions will require care. Some will need to be cleaned. Others will need to be restored. You will also need to know how to display your collectibles in the safest, most appealing way, and how to pack and ship them properly. This book discusses these issues in a straightforward, practical way.

Keep Accurate Records—Careful collectors also keep a detailed record of their acquisitions. This includes information on when and where each item was purchased, its price and the maker and date of manufacture. This book will show you how to set up a record book and how to photograph your mementos for historical and insurance purposes.

The 1940s and 1950s were known for sophisticated design and outlandish fads. A collection of memorabilia from this era might include examples of both, such as the Russell Wright dishes and Davy Crockett hat above.

Glossary

Advertiques—Items such as signs, trade cards and novelties used to promote or advertise products.

Aluminum—A lightweight, malleable and rust-resistant metal. It was widely used during the 1940s and 1950s for tableware, novelties and kitchen accessories.

Art Deco—Style of the 1920s, 1930s and 1940s characterized by streamlined shapes. Materials such as chrome and Bakelite were widely used.

Bakelite—A resin or plastic used to make small objects such as knobs for furniture. It is dense, hard and can be produced in many appealing colors.

Bamboo—Hard, knotty Oriental wood used for furniture during the 1950s.

Bentwood—Pieces of wood steamed until soft, then bent into various shapes.

Black glass—Term for opaque, dark-green bottle glass.

Black light—A fluorescent tube emitting ultraviolet radiation. When black light is directed on repaired or altered antiques or paintings, the alterations look different from the original material.

Box lot—A container holding a group of inexpensive items sold as a single lot at an auction.

Cane—A reedy plant from the East Indies used to make lightweight furniture.

Catalin—A brittle, brightly colored plastic used to make radios during the 1930s and 1940s.

Celluloid—An early plastic that was transparent, lightweight and fragile.

Ceramics—Objects such as vases or tableware made of pottery or porcelain.

Character toys—Toys, games or books modeled after or based on lives of famous movie, radio or television personalities.

China—See *Porcelain*.

Chrome—Metal, usually iron, coated with an alloy of the element chromium. Has a shiny, silver appearance.

Composition—Mixture of wood or paper pulp, sawdust, glue and water used to make household collectibles such as storage boxes, napkin holders, and salt and pepper shakers.

Console—A combination radio and phonogragh, or radio/phonograph/television, usually housed in the same cabinet.

Costume jewelry—Inexpensive jewelry made without jewels or precious metals that often resembles more expensive pieces.

Depression glass—Brightly colored, machine-pressed glass inexpensively produced from the 1930s to the 1950s. The term refers to the fact that this material first became popular during the Great Depression of the 1930s.

Display card—A large movie poster, usually about 22x28 inches. It is displayed in movie-house lobbies.

Ebonized—Wood that has been painted black to imitate ebony, a rare and expensive wood.

Fiberglass—Glass in a fibrous form used in 1950s furniture.

Frosted drinking glass—Glass covered with a white substance that disappears when a cold liquid is poured into the container, thus revealing a scene or figures (often naughty!) beneath the substance.

Go-withs—Objects such as boxes and instructional materials that relate to a collectible piece.

This advertique, a counter display, was one in a series of Parke, Davis & Co. promotional series called *A History of Pharmacy in Pictures*. Advertiques like this are increasingly popular and not easy to find. This one is a bargain at $10.

Handkerchief vase—An Italian, blown-glass vase of the 1950s whose shape resembles a handkerchief bunched at one end.

Industrial materials—Materials such as chrome, steel wire, plastics and glass that modern designers use for housewares and furniture.

Latex—Milky liquid from the rubber tree used to make many rubber products.

Leatherette—Plastic that is colored and embossed to resemble leather.

Logo—The mark of a manufacturer, usually initials or an abstract design.

Manufacturer's mark—Stamped, impressed, applied or labeled name of the maker of an object.

Memorabilia—Collectible items relating to a specific era or subject, such as the 1950s or a movie star.

Milk glass—Opaque white or blue glass used for novelties and tableware.

Modern School—A group of designers and architects of the 1920s, 1930s and 1940s who used industrial materials such as steel and plastic to produce sleek, streamlined buildings and furnishings.

Modular furniture—Sets of cabinets, shelves and other furniture designed to be joined in various ways or arranged as a group. Such furnishings were popular during the 1950s.

Neon—Colorless, odorless gas. Neon glows when it is sealed in a glass tube and an electric charge is passed through it.

Organic furniture—Furniture, usually wood, that takes its shape from the natural shape of the material it is made from. For example, the cross-section of a tree trunk could become a table.

Paste—A term used for glass imitations of precious stones such as diamonds or rubies.

Pastels—Pale colors, such as pink, light gray and green, that were especially popular during the 1950s.

Patina—Worn surface on an antique or collectible. Characterized by cracking paint, worn spots and fading.

Pedestal chair or table—A piece of modern furniture, often plastic, mounted on a narrow pedestal base.

Photographers' gum—Sticky, gumlike rubber substance used by photographers to hold objects together or to make them stand upright.

Plastics—Nonmetallic compounds that can be molded into various shapes. Plastics are flexible, lightweight and weather-resistant.

Plywood—Sheets of strong, flexible laminated wood. The grain of each sheet is glued at right angles to the next.

Polyurethanes—Hard and soft synthetic substances that can serve as substitutes for textiles, wood or metals.

Porcelain—A mixture of chemical ingredients that becomes a hard, transparent material when heated.

Pottery—Objects made from clays.

Premiums—Items such as toys, housewares and reading materials either given away with products or obtainable

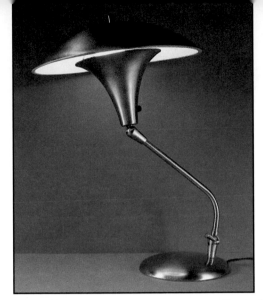

This adjustable chrome table lamp reflects the best design elements of the late 1950s. Made in limited quantities, it is worth $350 to $450.

through redeemable coupons.

Prop—An item used in the productions of a movie, stage play or television show.

Scandinavian Modern—Furniture style of the 1950s emphasizing simple flowing lines and minimal decoration. Most pieces were wood, glass or pottery, or a combination of these materials.

Shadow box—Picture frame with a deep rim on which objects are placed for display. May or may not be covered with glass.

Slag glass—Heavy, multicolored glass resembling marble.

Staffordshire—A pottery-making area of England. Small mantel decorations such as animals, banks and human figures are often referred to as *Staffordshire figures.*

Synthetics—Man-made materials, such as plastics, that replace natural materials in furniture construction.

Tortoise shell—A mottled brown-and-yellow material originally obtained from tortoise shells and used for purses, mirror backs, combs and other objects. During the 1940s and 1950s, imitation tortoise shell was made from plastics.

Tubular steel—Tin sheets of steel rolled into hollow tubes to create lightweight, flexible furniture-making material.

Vintage clothing—Collectors' term for collectible clothing. Formerly used only in reference to Victorian garments, the term now means authentic clothing from any era.

Vinyl—A plastic resin used to make phonograph records, accessories and furniture coverings.

Wicker—Woven rattan, bamboo or other imported vines or grasses used for lightweight furniture.

Zoot suit—Extravagantly styled men's suit of the late 1940s and early 1950s featuring an unusually long jacket with exaggerated lapels, and pants with wide cuffs.

Categories of Collectibles

Collecting is one of the last bastions of individualism. You don't have to go to school to learn how to be a collector. You don't have to follow any strict rules.

Most collectors are very independent. Even so, they usually establish some ground rules about collecting. This is especially important with any area as broad as 1940s and 1950s memorabilia.

In this field, collectors usually classify items by material, function or manufacturer.

COLLECTING BY MATERIAL

The material category is traditional. It includes plastics, metals, ceramics and glass. Some enthusiasts concentrate on subcategories, such as Depression glass or bamboo furniture.

COLLECTING BY FUNCTION

Collections based on the functions of mementos often reflect the enthusiast's interests and background. For example, a homemaker might buy kitchen collectibles. A movie fan might collect memorabilia associated with the stars of the 1940s and 1950s.

New collectors are often stunned by the number of items available. A collection of radios and televisions could fill an average-sized house. A small collection of Marilyn Monroe memorabilia would fill several scrapbooks—and would cost a great deal of money.

OVERLAPPING CATEGORIES

Many categories overlap. For example, if you decide to collect kitchen objects, you can buy glass, pottery and metal items. If you want movie memorabilia, you will purchase mementos made of paper, cardboard, glass, metal and wood.

Collectors follow few rules. You should acquire things you enjoy. Keep in mind your interests, lifestyle and pocketbook. Also think about the space you have available for your collection.

CREATING YOUR OWN CATEGORIES

If traditional collecting categories don't interest you, create your own. You can use these chapters as guides.

If your interests and tastes involve different areas such as ceramics and movie memorabilia combine them in the way that works best for you. For example, you could collect pottery mementos related to movies. Many such souvenirs are available.

When choosing a category, remember several important factors. How much can you spend on your collection? How large do you want it to be? How much display space is available? How rare are the items you want to collect? Thinking about these issues before you start collecting will save time and money.

COLLECTING EUROPEAN MEMENTOS

One decision you will have to make is whether to buy objects made in Europe. Some enthusiasts—such as those who collect toys or dolls—purchase many items made abroad. You don't have to do this if you decide to collect 1940s and 1950s memorabilia. Many items made in the United States are available. You can assemble an excellent collection without buying a single object manufactured in Europe.

So many American-made mementos are available that you could create an impressive collection of objects from one region of the country. You could specialize in chrome products manufactured by Midwestern factories, or radios made by Eastern firms.

The most important consideration in choosing a category is selecting one that reflects your personality and interests. That way, your collection will grow with you. It can become an important part of your life.

CHOOSING A CATEGORY

Nostalgia is a major reason many people collect 1940s and 1950s memorabilia. Most enthusiasts buy items they remember from their childhoods. Such mementos bring back memories of past experiences.

You may fondly recall Saturday afternoons when you watched cartoons and Abbott and Costello movies at the neighborhood cinema. Such recollections might lead you to purchase movie memorabilia.

Perhaps you remember setting the kitchen table with pink Depression glass. You might want to look for similar pieces now.

COLLECT WHAT YOU LIKE

Whatever category you choose, base your collection on objects you like. Even if your collection becomes a business, don't forget what prompted you to start it.

COLLECT WHAT YOU CAN AFFORD

Don't choose a category that is too expensive. Few people can afford to assemble a collection of jukeboxes. These items may cost more than $1,000 each.

Most 1940s and 1950s mementos are reasonably priced. You can find hundreds of interesting chrome, plastic or wood items for $25 to $50 apiece.

The display and storage space you have will also help determine what you collect. Don't buy early television sets or phonographs unless you have a large attic or basement. However, you could assemble a very large collection of plastic jewelry and store it in a corner of one room. Before you make a commitment to any type of collectible, think about how you could display and store your acquisitions. Display is important. Few collectors want to keep everything in boxes. They take pride in showing their mementos to family, friends and other enthusiasts.

Display and storage considerations play a role in the size of the objects you can collect. They also affect how many pieces you can collect. It is usually better to avoid too large a field of concentration. Don't try to collect one of every known piece of Depression glass. It would be exhausting, expensive and probably impossible. Instead, buy a single type of Depression glass. You could assemble a large, interesting collection of blue Moderntone or pale-green Patrician glass.

Avoid choosing a category that is too narrow. If you decide to collect rare radios, you may wait months or years to add a new item to your collection.

BUY QUALITY ITEMS

Always buy the best pieces you can afford. Look for old or rare items, or those in mint condition. Experienced collectors and dealers agree that buying the best will give you the greatest satisfaction and the highest return on your investment. Spending $10 on one good item is almost always better than spending $20 on five items. Ordinary and damaged collectibles will always be available. However, high-quality mementos may vanish or increase greatly in price.

Gaudy, printed wallpaper from the 1950s featured everything from animal orchestras to tropical fruits. If you find several rolls in a closet, they may be worth $50 to $200 each, depending on the patterns.

FURNITURE

If you decide to collect furniture from the 1940s and 1950s, your major problem will be limiting your acquisitions. That era was unique in American history. Millions of veterans returned home from World War II; married and established households. These men and their families purchased thousands of pieces of furniture. Much of it is still being used or is in storage, awaiting the arrival of collectors.

Furniture from this period was produced in various styles and materials, including steel, glass, plastic and wood.

THE MODERN SCHOOL

This variety reflected the attitudes of different furniture designers. Three groups of designers were especially popular.

These designers continued the sleek lines and spare look of the so-called *Modern School,* which had appeared in the United States before World War II. Modernists used industrial materials such as tubular steel, chrome, iron and glass. After the war they also used newer materials, including plastic, fiberglass and polyurethane.

THE DANISH SCHOOL

Another group of designers utilized the *Danish Modern,* or *Scandinavian Modern,* style. They rejected metal and plastic as cold and inappropriate for home furnishings. These designers worked with wood, especially laminated wood and bentwood. They believed in mass production and standardized designs.

HANDMADE FURNITURE

A third group rejected mass production. They preferred to create their furnishings by hand, one item at a time, just as craftsmen had done in ancient times. These designers produced relatively few pieces. Their work is hard to find and often more expensive than mass-produced furnishings.

Some collectors buy examples from all three schools. However, most enthusiasts purchase items in one style. This is an excellent way to limit your collection. You can also narrow your options by collecting pieces by one designer, or by acquiring furnishings made of one type of material.

This laminated plywood side chair by Charles Eames would be an excellent find for any collector. Manufactured during the late 1940s and 1950s, these chairs can be found throughout the United States. At $250 to $500 each, they are worth looking for!

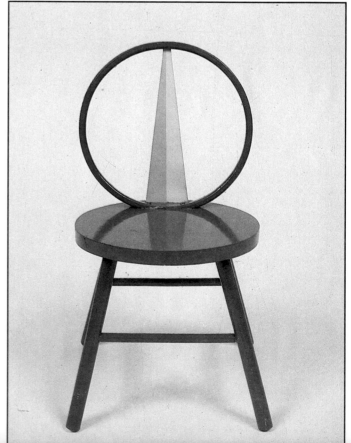

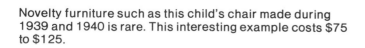

Novelty furniture such as this child's chair made during 1939 and 1940 is rare. This interesting example costs $75 to $125.

This Art Deco-style bamboo armchair has large cushions with a bold tropical pattern. Such patterns were very popular during the 1940s and 1950s. Originally designed as porch furniture, bamboo chairs and tables are now seen throughout fashionable homes. This armchair is worth $150 to $250.

Aluminum furnishings became popular after World War II. This aluminum-and-leather stool was designed by Donald Deskey, who was famous for his Art Deco furnishings. This piece was produced between 1935 and 1955. It costs $175 to $235.

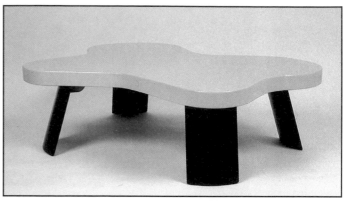

Paul Frankl created this unusual lacquered mahogany-and-pine coffee table. It was made from 1949 until 1960 and costs $500 to $750.

You may have had a tubular-steel, vinyl-upholstered settee in your living room. This item was designed by Gilbert Rohde and was made between 1935 and 1950. It is worth $200 to $250 in good condition. Remember that condition is a crucial factor in determining price.

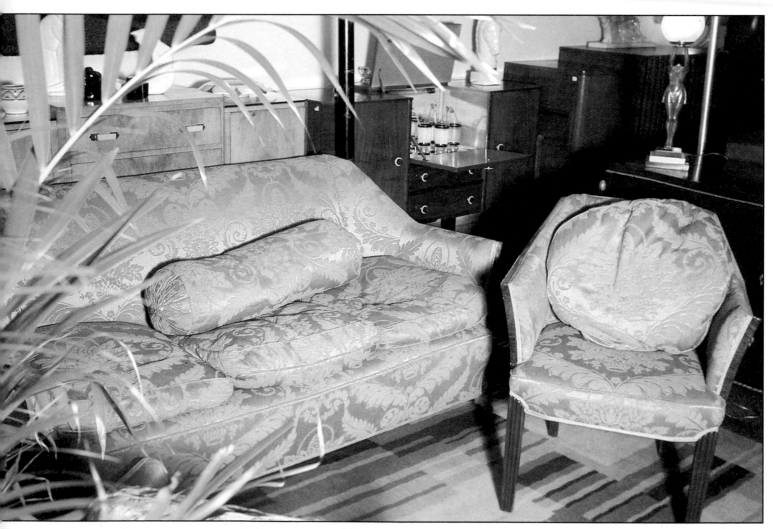

A typical 1940s living room. The upholstered couch costs $300 to $400, and the matching armchair is $125 to $165. Upholstery repair is very expensive, so buy furnishings such as these only if they are in good condition.

This maple-and-mahogany glass-top dressing table was produced during the late 1930s and 1940s by a Midwestern manufacturer. It was designed by Gilbert Rohde. A high-quality example such as this costs $500 to $800.

COLLECTING BY DESIGNER

If you want your collection to be not only a hobby but also an investment, purchase the work of specific furniture designers.

Many designers of this period were innovative. They had been trained in architecture or industrial design. Some were so well-respected that their names appeared with the manufacturer's mark on the furnishings. Others created unique pieces that can be recognized even if unmarked.

Names such as Saarinen, Rohde and Esherick may not be household words, but they are well-known among collectors and dealers. Furnishings by these designers bring high prices.

Let's look at an example. In 1946, a well-known designer named Charles Eames created a simple side chair of tubular steel and plywood. It was first manufactured in 1947 by the Herman Miller Co. of Zeeland, Michigan. It was labeled *Herman Miller/Evans/Charles Eames.*

This chair was so popular that it was produced for years and became known as the *Eames chair.* Most later examples differed slightly and were not labeled the same way.

Today, a 1947 example may cost more than $1,000. Similar chairs manufactured later cost less than $100! It pays to know about manufacturers and the history of furniture-making.

Several designers are especially popular with dealers and collectors.

Charles Eames (1907-1979) — This designer was associated with the Herman Miller Co. of Michigan. Eames created furnishings in laminated wood and bentwood. He often combined these materials with steel bases. He also made molded polyester chairs shaped like shells.

Eero Saarinen (1910-1961) — He was associated with Knoll International Inc., of New York City. He is best-known for his famous *womb chair,* a molded plastic shell covered with upholstery and mounted on a polished steel frame. He also designed plastic and cast-aluminum pedestal chairs and tables.

Harry Bertoia (1915-1978) — Bertoia, who had trained as a sculptor, was also associated with Knoll. He twisted iron wire into fancifully shaped chairs, tables, couches, lamp stands and other objects.

Gilbert Rohde (1894-1944) — During his association with the Herman Miller Co., Rohde created many pieces that combined traditional woods such as mahogany and maple with industrial materials such as chrome and glass. His work often blended the elements of the modern movement with those of Art Deco.

Wharton Esherick (1887-1970) — He may have been the first 20th-century designer to promote one-of-a-kind, handcrafted furnishings. He is famous for his abstract, sculptural furniture. Many pieces were built from hundreds of tiny blocks of wood, glued together and then cut and sanded into strange, sinuous shapes.

George Nakashima (1905-) —This designer used natural materials. He thought of them as whole units rather than building blocks. He built chairs and tables from tree trunks. This type of furniture is often called *organic.*

These are just a few well-known designers. As you read, visit dealers and go to museum exhibitions, you will learn about others. You may discover you especially admire one designer and want to collect that person's work.

The important thing to remember is that furniture by famous designers and manufacturers is increasing in value. Unidentifiable furnishings or items made by designers whose names have not yet attracted collectors' attention are much less expensive.

COLLECTING FURNITURE BY TYPE

You can approach furniture collecting many different ways. You could buy furnishings made of one type of material, such as wood, plastic, steel, glass or combinations of these. You could buy various examples of specific types of furnishings, such as chairs or beds.

Create a Period Decor —One advantage of collecting these items is that you can furnish your home with them. After all, 40-year-old furnishings are not antiques. They don't have to be treated any special way. If you like things from the 1940s and 1950s, live with them!

Many furnishings from this era are better-made than contemporary pieces. They may also be more valuable. Contemporary furnishings lose 70% of their value as soon as you take them out of the store. Pieces from the 1940s and 1950s are continually appreciating.

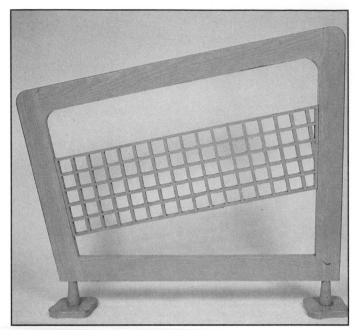

This oak room divider is relatively rare. Made between 1945 and 1955, it has a sculptural look appealing to contemporary collectors. It is worth $250 to $350.

Made of woven plastic over an iron-rod frame, this child's rocker costs $50 to $75. It was manufactured during the 1950s and is widely available.

Glass and tubular-steel or stainless-steel tea carts were made from 1930 until the mid-1950s. Their manufacturers usually cannot be identified. This tea cart costs $75 to $150.

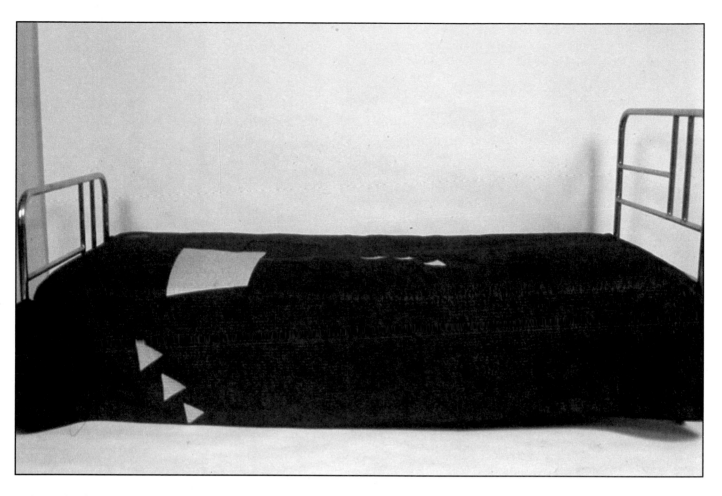

This tubular-steel single bed is a modern version of the familiar antique brass bed. Although not as valuable as its brass counterpart, this bed is worth $200 to $300. It was made between 1944 and 1955.

This small, laminated wood stool by Charles Eames was produced in the early 1950s. It is worth $200 to $250.

Buy Items in Good Condition—Because furniture from this era is so readily available and inexpensive, you should be choosy. Buy the best examples you can find. Such items should have a stamped, labeled, imprinted or impressed manufacturer's mark and should be in excellent condition.

Don't buy damaged specimens or those requiring extensive reupholstering or restoration. If you do buy damaged furniture, make sure it is so unusual that the additional expense is justified.

Look for Manufacturers' Marks—Be sure to check for manufacturers' marks before you buy an item. Such marks can usually be found inside drawers, on the backs of cupboards and desks, under the tops of tables, and on metal fittings such as hinges and locks.

Study Design Techniques—Learn to recognize unmarked pieces. Labels fall off. If you are familiar with the lines and construction methods used in pieces by Bertoia or Nakashima, you will be able to recognize these furnishings even when they are unmarked.

This skill will set you apart from the average collector and can help you find excellent bargains. Study old catalogs and furnishings in antique shops, museum collections and books.

Familiarize yourself with the style and materials used by different designers.

COLLECTING 1940s AND 1950s FURNITURE

Collectors think this category is exciting because so many types of furnishings are available. Some furniture dealers in cities such as New York, Chicago and Los Angeles specialize in pieces from the 1940s and 1950s. Such dealers charge high prices. They usually handle the rarest, most choice items and set prices accordingly.

Check Used-Furniture Stores—Thousands of pieces of furniture from this era are available in used-furniture stores. Other pieces are listed in the classified-ad sections of local newspapers. If you are persistent, you can find wonderful examples at a fraction of what they would cost if purchased from a major dealer.

Attend Auctions—You can sometimes get bargains at auctions, especially auctions of household goods. Most estate sales include furniture from the 1940s and 1950s. However, knowledgeable auctioneers or buyers will sometimes force prices up.

Advertise Locally—The best technique for locating furniture is to advertise in local papers. Although most people don't recognize Chippendale or Arts and Crafts furniture, they do remember the furnishings of 40 years ago.

Advertising can produce excellent results. You might pay $20 to $50 for a piece that a knowledgeable dealer would charge $200 to $1,000 for. And your neighbors will be pleased to get a "white elephant" off their hands.

BUYING AND SELLING FURNITURE

• Designers are important. Buy furnishings that are functional and will increase in value.
• Buy pieces with manufacturers' marks or unmarked items recognizable as the work of important furniture designers such as Eames, Bertoia, Esherick or Rohde.
• Don't purchase furnishings by lesser-known designers. Such pieces may cost less now, but they will not appreciate in value as rapidly as pieces by famous designers.
• Avoid extensively restored or refinished pieces.
• Many furnishings from the 1940s and 1950s have been completely repainted or refinished in colors or finishes that differ from those used originally. As collectors become more sophisticated, they will reject such pieces.

A remarkable piece of furniture by any standard, this folding screen from the 1950s was designed by Gio Ponti. It costs $2,500 to $3,500.

European furnishings made between 1940 and 1950 are often more expensive than their American counterparts. This walnut desk with cast-bronze legs was created by the famous Italian designer Gio Ponti. It is valued at $2,500 to $3,000.

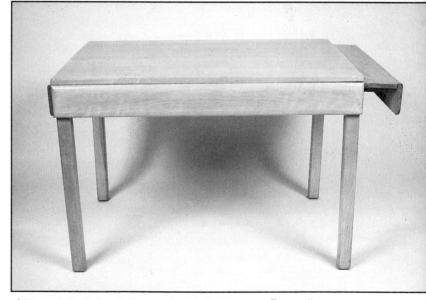

Although he is best-known for his tableware, Russell Wright also designed furniture. This bleached-maple expandable dining table was produced from the late 1930s until the late 1940s. Its value is $350 to $750. Pieces by well-known furniture designers are worth more than those created by lesser-known figures.

RADIOS, PHONOGRAPHS, JUKEBOXES AND TELEVISION SETS

Entertainment devices are interesting—and expensive—collectibles. Prices range from $30 to $50 for an ordinary 1950s phonograph to more than $10,000 for a rare 1940s jukebox.

This field has a limited number of collectors. Most examples that enthusiasts find on their own are not in working order. Such items usually require extensive restoration that may cost hundreds of dollars. Restoration is necessary, however. Few enthusiasts are interested in nonworking jukeboxes or television sets.

Most collectors buy working examples from dealers or other enthusiasts. Such mementos are usually expensive.

One of the most popular collectibles of the 1940s and 1950s is the plastic-cased radio. This Hallicrafters Continental table model is valued at $60 to $75 in working condition. Look for examples in red, green or blue.

RADIOS

Radios were manufactured in great quantities after World War I. Examples made during the late 1930s and 1940s are especially popular with collectors. Made of *Bakelite* or *Catalin,* another early type of plastic, these radios had four to six tubes. They were seldom more than 14 inches long and 10 inches high.

Bakelite radios are attractive because of their styles and colors. Most were produced in a sleek, Art Deco style. They feature spectacular molded shapes and bold colors. Many were red, blue, green, custard yellow, white, maroon, orange or combinations of these colors. Rare examples had a marbleized surface or were embellished with bits of chrome and blue glass.

Color is important. Brown Bakelite radios are worth much less than models in other colors. A red Bakelite radio might cost $150. The same model in brown might cost $25.

Many different manufacturers produced these radios. They include RCA, Bendix, Motorola, GE, Crosley, Fada, Emerson and Arvin. Most enthusiasts are not concerned with the manufacturer. They are concerned with appearance. And what appearances these radios have! Some are shaped like skyscrapers. A few resemble Mayan temples. Some remind us of old-time automobiles. Others look like refrigerators. Their colors and designs resemble the Westinghouse refrigerators on which they sat.

PHONOGRAPHS

Most phonograph collectors are interested only in the hand-cranked, spring-driven models of the late 19th and early 20th centuries. Therefore, people who want to collect phonographs of the late 1930s and 1940s have no problem finding excellent examples.

If you are interested in phonographs, remember that many records, such as rare examples by popular singers of the time, may be worth more than the phonographs on which they were played!

Explore the possibility of collecting portables. These were very popular during this era. Early high-fidelity components appeared soon after World War II, replacing the standard self-contained system.

JUKEBOXES

Don't try collecting jukeboxes unless you have a great deal of money or are a mechanic skilled in restoration. Functioning jukeboxes from the 1940s and early 1950s cost from $3,000 to $10,000. Prices depend on rarity, condition and appearance. Collectors compete for prime examples with bars and restaurants that install jukeboxes in nostalgic settings.

The term *jukebox* comes from *juke,* meaning *disorder* in the dialect of the Gullah, a group of blacks from western Africa. It is unclear how this term came to refer to these large, coin-operated devices. The word certainly fits, however. Many early jukeboxes sound "disorderly" because their giant built-in speakers magnify sound. The devices also have overblown Art Deco styling, with oak veneer, chrome-plated frames and neon tubes. Bubbles pulsate through the tubes, as if trying to keep time to the music.

Although jukeboxes appeared before World War II, their heyday was the late 1940s and the 1950s. They were then gradually replaced by smaller versions that had a central sound system.

Wurlitzer and Chantel were major jukebox manufacturers. Wurlitzer made dozens of models. All are now collectible.

TELEVISION SETS

The first television receiver was introduced by RCA Victor at the 1939 World's Fair in New York City.

World War II prevented development in this field until the mid-1940s. Television sets became generally available in the 1950s.

Early sets reflected the received image from a mirror mounted on the underside of a hinged lid. For years the image appeared on a 4x6-inch, or slightly larger, field. Magnifying plates increased the size of the image. These plates and sets are collectible.

Values fluctuate greatly. Study the field before you buy. Remember, not many collectors are interested in televisions. Although an early or rare set might cost more than $1,000, many sets made in the late 1940s and 1950s cost less than $100. Don't pay too much.

Look for early consoles in which a television set was combined with a phonograph or radio, or both. Some of these are rare and will increase in value.

COLLECTING RADIOS, PHONOGRAPHS, JUKEBOXES AND TELEVISION SETS

One of the best ways to find these items is to look in the back rooms of shops that repair electronic equipment.

Many repairmen have old equipment that was used for trade-ins or was left for repair and never claimed.

Ask Wholesalers and Retailers—Wholesale and retail dealers of radios and television sets may also have older models.

Attend Yard Sales—Also check yard sales. Many people will not even display old TVs, radios and phonographs that don't function. They think such items have no value. Be sure to ask whether old models are stored in the attic or basement. Be sure to explain that you don't expect the device to work.

Many dealers have Bakelite radios. Few have jukeboxes, phonographs or television sets from the 1940s and 1950s.

Be Careful About Repairs—Making repairs can be expensive. Few radios, phonographs, jukeboxes or television sets that have been stored for long periods will work. When you buy these items, keep in mind the possible repair bill. If you think it will be too high, look for a similar item in better condition.

Always get written estimates for restoration or repair work. They will help you avoid misunderstandings and additional expense.

Dealers usually sell models in working order. This means you pay for the repair work they have done. It is not unusual to pay $200 or more for some types of plastic radios that have been restored. Jukeboxes in working condition cost even more.

BUYING AND SELLING RADIOS, PHONOGRAPHS, JUKEBOXES AND TELEVISION SETS

- Prices for jukeboxes are too high for the average collector.
- Bakelite radios cost hundreds of dollars. However, radios in wood cases are inexpensive. Many are very attractive, with cabinets resembling Gothic churches.
- Most phonographs are inexpensive.
- Most early television sets are also reasonably priced. These sets are often excellent bargains. They are interesting, readily available and will increase in value.

Prices for television sets are increasing. This plastic-cased Sylvania Dualette, made from 1955 to 1960, is worth $100 to $150 in working condition.

POTTERY

If you like pottery, you will find plenty to collect from the 1940s and 1950s. Ceramics factories involved in the war effort during the early 1940s returned to peacetime production at the end of World War II. They produced pottery in amazing quantities. One firm, the Hull Pottery Co. of Crooksville, Ohio, made more than 3 million pieces a year during the late 1940s!

Pottery made during this era falls into two broad collecting categories that often overlap. These categories are table settings and ceramic novelties.

Table Settings—This category includes plates, cups and saucers, and serving dishes. Perhaps the most popular manufacturer of such items was the Homer Laughlin Co. of Newell, West Virginia. This firm made the Fiesta and Harlequin lines, which sold very well.

Other collectors prefer the dishware designed by Russell Wright.

Ceramic Novelties—These included large table lamps shaped like leopards or deer, and pottery cookie jars produced by the Hull Co. or the McCoy Pottery Co. of Roseville, Ohio.

If you are a beginning pottery collector, keep several factors in mind.

Quality—The more complete your groupings, the more valuable they will be. A complete set of Fiesta in yellow will be more valuable than the same number of pieces in several different hues. A complete set in a rare shade, such as red, will be even more valuable.

Limit Your Collection—You can't collect even a fraction of the available pieces. Most enthusiasts concentrate on acquiring one brand, such as Frankoma or Shawnee. Others collect different examples of a specific item, such as cookie jars.

Be Choosy—Whatever approach you use, remember that with few exceptions, ceramics of this era are plentiful and inexpensive. This means you can be choosy. Don't buy damaged pieces and don't pay high prices. If you are patient, you will find a similar piece that will be in better condition and will cost less.

Several dozen potteries were active during the 1940s and 1950s. Collectors are interested in the products of fewer than a dozen. Background information provided in this section will help you decide how to tailor your collection.

FIESTA WARE

This colorful, modernistic tableware was manufactured by the Homer Laughlin Co. from 1936 until 1969. Although Fiesta is regarded as a product of the 1930s, it was most popular during 1950s, when a line of pastel colors was introduced. For years, collectors favored the darker hues. Now enthusiasts are looking for Fiesta pieces in pink, gray, pale green and other pastels.

Each of these green ceramic serving bowls has Russell Wright's mark. These bowls are $35 to $50 each. They were made during the 1940s.

This finely crafted porcelain figure of an African woman was made between 1955 and 1965. Valued between $135 and $185, this piece is reminiscent of Art Deco works.

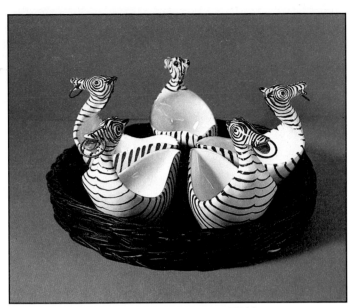

This set of Italian ceramic nut dishes comes in a woven wicker tray. Each piece is marked *ITALY.* The bold stripes were used in many European designs during the 1950s. The set is valued at $90 to $120. Individual dishes are $15 to $20.

Most Fiesta was marked on the bottom with some variation of the logo *FIESTA/HLC U.S.A.* Unmarked pieces can be recognized by the concentric circles in the centers of plates and saucers. Cups and beakers have decorative rings around the rims.

Standard Fiesta colors include red; ivory; dark blue; light, medium and dark green; yellow; rose; turquoise; gray; chartreuse; and red-orange.

Most collectors look for pieces in dark blue and red. Such items are expensive. Red is especially rare, because one component of the hue was uranium oxide. The U.S. government used this material from 1943 to 1959, making it unavailable to manufacturers.

Some pastel shades are also hard to find. Specific pieces may be rare in some shades. A divided or compartment plate has never been found in chartreuse.

Most Fiesta pieces cost $3 to $10 each. Rare examples cost hundreds of dollars. Knowledgeable collectors are trying to acquire complete table settings of popular pastels, such as ivory and gray.

The black leopard was a popular figure in the 1950s. Examples varied from 6 inches to 3 feet in length. The larger figure here is 14 inches long and is worth $125 to $150. The smaller leopard is 12 inches long and costs $75 to $100.

HARLEQUIN

Harlequin, also made by Homer Laughlin, was a less-expensive version of Fiesta. Colors and basic shapes are similar. Harlequin pieces are more elongated and have sharper angles. The decorative rings around the tops of saucers and pitchers don't reach the rims of the vessels. Plates and saucers do not have concentric circles in the middle. Harlequin pieces are never marked.

Harlequin was sold mostly through the Woolworth chain. It cost about 20% to 30% less than Fiesta. It is also less expensive today, because collectors prefer Fiesta.

LU-RAY PASTELS

Another neglected line of tableware has *LU-RAY PASTELS/USA* marked on the base of each piece. This tableware was made in several pastel shades, including gray, pale blue, pale green, pink and yellow. Lu-Ray pieces are an excellent buy. You can often purchase individual examples for $1. It is not unusual to purchase a plate for 25 cents or 50 cents at a yard sale. The sleek lines of these pieces are typical of tableware made during the 1940s and 1950s. Lu-Ray pastels are ideal for the beginning collector.

RUSSELL WRIGHT

Russell Wright is one of the best modern designers. His work in glass, plastics, textiles and furniture is well-known. To most collectors, Russell Wright is synonymous with a line of sleek, ultramodern pottery.

Wright worked for several firms. His best-known line was American Modern. He designed it for the Steubenville (Ohio) Pottery Co., which produced it from 1939 to 1959. This tableware was enhanced by flowing lines and exaggerated handles and spouts. It came in hues with such distinctive names as Bean Brown, Seafoam Blue, Black Chutney, Cantaloupe and Cedar Green.

Other Russell Wright pottery was produced by the Iroquois China Co. from 1946 to 1960, and the Harker Chinaware Co. of East Liverpool, Ohio, from 1951 to 1955. The style of this tableware was bold. The colors were described in unusual terms. The Iroquois line came in Sugar White, Ripe Apricot and Pink sherbert. Colors for the White Clover line made by Harker included Coral Sand and Golden Spree.

Wright's pottery is becoming more valuable. You can still find a table setting—a dinner plate, cup and saucer, bread and butter plate, soup bowl and salad plate—for less than $30 in a common color such as pink.

Many hotels ordered imprinted china in popular styles of the era. Such pieces are especially collectible. Those shown above are valued at $20 to $30 each.

The same set in Cedar Green could cost $100. Accessories are more expensive. A carafe may cost $50, and large casseroles may bring $25 to $40.

Fiesta tableware is inexpensive and appealing. The deep plate costs $10 to $15, and the cream-soup cup is $12 to $18. Look for rare colors, such as cobalt blue and deep red.

HULL POTTERY

Some collectors believe decorative pieces and novelties are more interesting than tableware. Many of these enthusiasts collect cookie jars and other pieces produced by the Hull Co.

This firm was established in 1917. Collectors acquire pieces made between 1940 and 1952, the year the firm closed. Hull's best-known line is Little Red Riding Hood. It included cookie jars, salt and pepper shakers, teapots, creamers and sugar bowls shaped like the red-caped, fairy-tale heroine.

Hull produced many other pieces during the 1940s. These included planters, pitchers and novelty items.

Many items are reasonably priced. However, a Red Riding Hood cookie jar costs $150 to $200. A similar piece shaped like Goldilocks sells for about half that.

McCOY POTTERY

Another 1950s manufacturer of novelty pieces was the McCoy Pottery Co. These items, marked *McCoy* on the bottom, included mugs, planters, vases and banks. McCoy also made a line of cookie jars featuring fairy-tale and cartoon characters.

Frankoma Pottery of Sapulpa, Oklahoma was another popular manufacturer. This pitcher was made about 1950 and costs $12 to $18. It is marked *FRANKOMA*.

Most McCoy pieces are excellent bargains. They cost $5 to $20 apiece. Look for a cookie jar shaped like an Indian. This rare item is worth more than $100.

SHAWNEE POTTERY

Exotic shapes are the hallmark of 1940s and 1950s ceramic novelty items. Many enthusiasts interested in such items collect pieces by Shawnee of Zanesville, Ohio. This firm operated from about 1935 to 1961 and produced two lines. They were the Corn King and Corn Queen. Each featured tableware, serving dishes and accessories shaped like ears of corn and glazed in green and yellow. Pieces are marked *SHAWNEE/USA.*

Both lines included ashtrays, bookends, planters, candleholders and cookie jars. Prices are very reasonable. Most pieces cost less than $25.

FRANKOMA POTTERY

The Frankoma Pottery of Sapulpa, Oklahoma, was founded in 1933. It is still in business. The company has produced dishware and novelty items. Many of these pieces interest collectors. Marked *FRANKOMA,* these items have Western motifs, such as wagon wheels, cacti and desert flowers. Glaze colors include tan, green and other Western hues.

Pieces also come in several shapes, including horses, dogs and leopards.

Frankoma ware is plentiful and moderately priced. Most pieces cost less than $50.

RED WING POTTERY

Red Wing Potteries of Red Wing, Minnesota, made numerous interesting pieces during the 1940s and 1950s. Most were marked *REDWING/USA.* They included serving dishes and accessory pieces. Cookie jars were made in several shapes, including a rooster, and a chef in apron and high hat. Some examples cost more than $100. Most are reasonably priced.

OCCUPIED-JAPAN CERAMICS

During the American occupation of Japan after World War II, the Japanese pottery industry was rebuilt and produced a remarkable variety of collectible ceramics. They are marked with some variation of the phrase, *Made in Occupied Japan.* The pieces range from fine porcelain dinnerware to copies of Staffordshire mantel figures. Japanese firms made hundreds of different salt and pepper sets, and novelty items featuring cartoon characters and historical figures.

This cup and saucer have the mark of Lu-Ray Pastels, a company that produced modernistic tableware in blue, green, pink, gray, yellow and white. Still moderately priced at $2 to $3 for the cup and $1 to $2 for the saucer, Lu-Ray Pastels are excellent buys for beginning collectors. These pieces date from the 1950s.

This child's bank was manufactured between 1950 and 1960 by the McCoy Pottery Co. of Roseville, Ohio. It costs $7 to $10. McCoy was one of the most important producers of contemporary ceramics.

These companies also copied French and German china. Some pieces have manufacturers' marks. The majority are identified only by the telltale label, *Occupied Japan.* That is the mark most collectors look for.

Collectors of pottery made in Occupied Japan usually concentrate on acquiring a single type of item. They may buy figures of children or animals. However, even after collectors narrow their options this way, they still have hundreds of pieces to choose from.

Pottery made in Occupied Japan is becoming more expensive. Large or rare pieces may cost more than $100. Ordinary specimens cost $10 to $35. A few years ago such pieces cost a few pennies.

COLLECTING POTTERY

Ceramics made during the 1940s and 1950s are popular and plentiful.

Talk With Dealers—Most antique and collectibles dealers have good selections. If you don't find what you want, tell the dealers about the items you are looking for. When they find such pieces, they will set them aside for you.

Go to Auctions—Many auction houses also handle collectibles from this period. You can find good bargains this way. Be sure to check the box lots at small auctions. These often contain interesting items that you can buy inexpensively.

Try Yard Sales and Bazaars—Attend yard sales and church bazaars. Many people are not aware of the new interest in 1940s and 1950s collectibles. They sell items made during this time very inexpensively or donate such items to charity. You may find a $50 item for $1 or $2.

Join Collectors' Clubs—Collectors of Fiesta Ware, Occupied Japan wares, and Red Wing and Frankoma pottery have established clubs. These organizations can help you learn more about what you are collecting. They also provide a network for collectors to buy, sell and trade items.

Advertise—Some collectors' groups publish newsletters. Such publications are good places to advertise for items you want. You can also place ads in your local newspapers and in collectors' publications, such as *Hobbies* and *The Antiques Trader.*

Before buying an advertised item, be sure to get a good description of it. Ceramics are easily chipped and cracked. What might appear to be a minor flaw to the seller can be a major drawback for the buyer. Ask for the right to return the piece if you are not satisfied.

BUYING AND SELLING POTTERY

- The big name in tableware is Russell Wright. Prices are increasing, but good buys are available.
- Try to obtain complete place settings.
- Buy as many pieces in one style as possible. The more complete the set, the more valuable it will be.
- Don't purchase single pieces from different sets. If you want to do this, buy creamers or cups and saucers. These items are recognized as individual collectibles.
- Look for interesting vases and pitchers from lesser-known manufacturers. Prices are lower, and if that manufacturer becomes popular, you could make an excellent profit.

The Art Deco style continued in ceramics well into the 1940s. This "jazzy" looking bowl was made by the famous Weller art pottery company around 1940. Its value is $25 to $35.

Cobalt blue is a collector favorite in Fiesta. This demitasse cup and saucer from the 1940s would probably bring $17 to $25 in blue—much less in most other colors.

Teapots shaped like birds and animals are always popular. This rooster was made by Red Wing Potteries of Red Wing, Minnesota. It is worth $20 to $30. The teapot was manufactured between 1940 and 1950.

GLASS

In the 1930s, glassware collectors concentrated on purchasing Depression and Heisey glass. Enthusiasts had dozens of examples to choose from, but never felt overwhelmed.

AMERICAN AND EUROPEAN GLASS

This situation changed in the 1940s. American manufacturers continued producing popular types of glassware. Many examples of Depression glass were made during the 1940s and 1950s. American designers also experimented with new forms.

Meanwhile, European and Scandinavian designers created a new line of glassware. It featured sleek or starkly geometric forms in bold, surrealistic colors. Collectors interested in glassware from this era have an enormous variety of examples to choose from.

Great advances in glass technology were made during this time. The manufacturers of Depression glass had produced items resistant to sudden temperature changes. This meant soup bowls, cups and coffeepots could be made of glass. Shatter-resistant glass also became available.

In addition, manufacturers learned to produce larger items. They made oblong planters, foot-long ashtrays, and table lamps shaped like rearing horses and movie celebrities. This tendency to produce large pieces may have reflected the general feeling of well-being and confidence that existed in the United States during the 1940s and 1950s.

Throughout the 1920s and 1930s, most glass was mass-produced. Few glassmakers made hand-blown, one-of-a-kind pieces. Many collectors feared that such craftsmanship would vanish. However, after World War II, European and American craftsmen began to produce free-blown art glass. Such items are much more expensive than machine-made glass. Today, collectors can purchase a factory-made product for $5 to $10, or a handcrafted rarity for $1,000.

LIMIT YOUR COLLECTION

You should limit your collection. Some enthusiasts buy Depression-glass table settings. Others acquire tumblers and glasses with decal decorations of palm trees, nudes or geometric designs. These were often sold as containers for processed-cheese spreads. Examples used for Kraft Food Co. products are referred to by collectors as *swanky swigs*.

Glass Figurines—Many collectors specialize in glass

The slim lines of these wooden-stoppered, milk-glass bar bottles reflect late-1950s styling. The pair would be reasonably priced at $30 to $45.

This pair of Venetian glass figurines costs $125 to $175. Similar pieces have been made for centuries on the Italian island of Murano. American tourists brought back many examples during the 1950s.

figurines. These items were produced in great quantities during this period. Most are fairly small, but foot-high figures—including some of Elvis Presley—were also made. Most figurines are clear glass or crystal. Some pieces have gilded or enameled decoration. Others are made of colored glass.

Most mold-formed examples were made in the United States. Hand-formed items may have been produced in Europe or Japan.

Collecting by Manufacturer—You might want to collect items made by one manufacturer. Many enthusiasts purchase examples from one or more of the important American glass factories. This is easy to do. Many items from the 1940s and 1950s are marked. Others can be identified by looking at sales catalogs and advertising materials.

The manufacturers whose products have attracted the most attention among collectors are included in this book. You can find some excellent bargains by looking for pieces by less-popular firms.

HEISEY GLASS

The A.H. Heisey Co. of Newark, Ohio, produced some of the most popular postwar glass before it closed in 1956. The firm's design was so advanced that in 1950, examples were exhibited at the Metropolitan Museum of Art in New York City. Heisey products are often marked with an *H* inside a diamond. The company imitated the expensive cut glass of the period, and made items in clear and colored glass. Rare examples, such as punch bowl sets and some figurines, cost hundreds of dollars. Most pieces can be purchased for $15 to $75.

LATE-DEPRESSION GLASS

Several firms continued to make the popular pressed glass after 1940. Collectors should look for several specific patterns:

Harp and Holiday—These patterns are by the Jeannette Glass Co. of Jeannette, Pennsylvania. Harp was made from 1954 to 1957. Holiday was made from 1947 to 1949.

Moonstone and Sandwich—Anchor Hocking Glass Corp. of Lancaster, Ohio, made these patterns. Moonstone was produced from 1941 to 1946. Sandwich was made from 1939 to 1964.

Heritage—The Federal Glass Co. of Columbus, Ohio, made this line during the 1940s and 1950s.

WESTMORLAND GLASS

The Westmorland Glass Co. of Grapeville, Pennsylvania, produced appealing novelty items during this period. These included high hats, pistols, shell-shaped compotes and an ashtray shaped like a turtle. These items were made of black, ruby and amber glass. Those made after 1949 are marked with the intertwined letters *W* and *G*.

PILGRIM GLASS

The Pilgrim Glass Co. of Ceredo, West Virginia, was established in 1951. It made fine-quality cranberry glass. The company produced a general line and one-of-a-kind studio pieces. Vases and paperweights usually had a paper label. They are popular collectibles.

DUNBAR GLASS

The Dunbar Glass Co. of Dunbar, West Virginia, is best-known for its beverage sets, cake stands, tumblers and vases. Collectors are also interested in the company's small animal figurines. Dunbar went out of business in 1953.

NEW MARTINSVILLE GLASS

Black glass was produced during the 1940s by the New Martinsville Glass Manufacturing Co. in West Virginia. Collectors are very interested in these items. New Martinsville's pieces had bold, modern shapes. The firm's products included perfume bottles and bowls. In 1944 New Martinsville became the Viking Glass Co. This firm's products are also collectible.

CRYSTAL GLASS

This glass was made at the Crystal Art Glass Factory in Cambridge, Ohio. The glass is called *Degenhart,* the name of the firm's owners.

The factory produced primarily novelty items. These included paperweights, salt and pepper shakers, toothpick holders, covered dishes shaped like birds and animals, and small vases.

Many items were made of rich, opaque slag glass in amethyst and off-white. These pieces are popular collectibles.

The company began production in 1947 and continued through the 1950s. Early examples are usually not marked.

McKEE GLASS

The McKee Glass Co. of Jeannette, Pennsylvania, produced many different types of collectible glass during the 1940s and early 1950s. Milk glass was one of the firm's specialties. It also made bar and utility glass in such exotic shades as Seville Yellow and Skokie Green.

SMITH GLASS

The largest producer of black-glass collectibles was the L.E. Smith Glass Co. of Mount Pleasant, Pennsylvania. During the 1940s this firm made very fanciful figural glass pieces. They included rearing horses, geese, dogs, cats, cows and squirrels. Smith marked its pieces with paper labels or with an embossed *C* in a circle, accompanied by a much smaller *s*. The company is still in business.

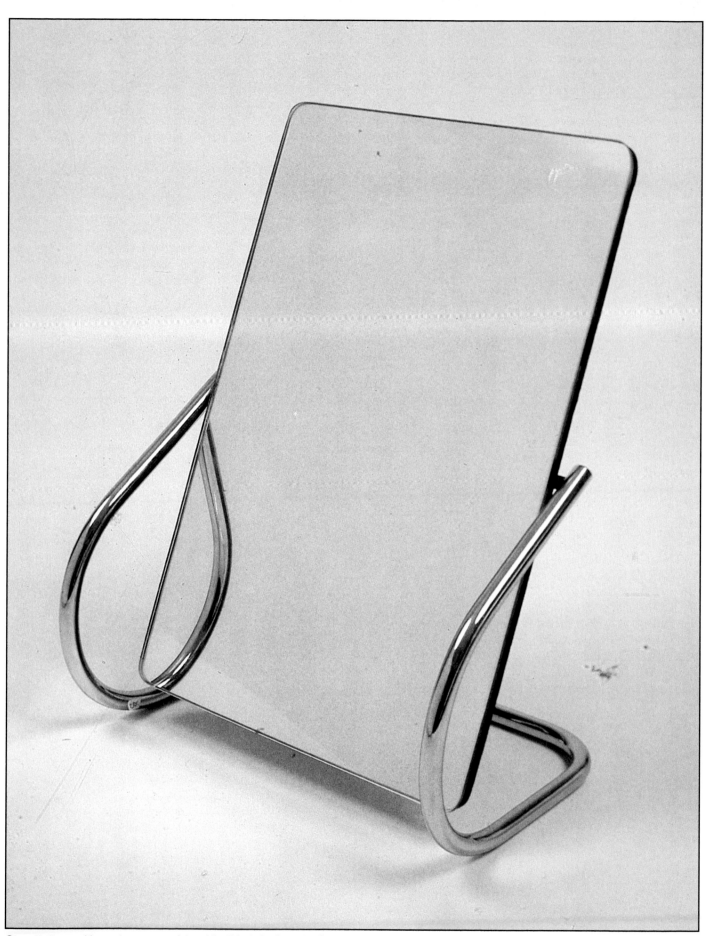

Simplicity and beauty are combined in this tubular-steel
and glass vanity mirror made during the 1950s. Such
mirrors are becoming rare. Examples in good condition
bring $45 to $70.

KANAWHA GLASS

The Kanawha Glass Co. of Dunbar, West Virginia, has produced a distinctive, heavy-bodied glass since 1955. This glass has an unusual *crackled,* or wrinkled, surface. Beverage, juice and tumbler sets have been manufactured in about two-dozen colors. Dunbar has also produced glass novelties. Look for pieces in the firm's red-yellow hue.

PADEN CITY GLASS

The Paden City Glass Manufacturing Co. of Paden City, West Virginia, was famous for its hand-shaped bowls, candlesticks, compotes and goblets. They were produced in exotic shades of red, opal, ebony and green until 1951.

These are a few of the more popular American glass factories active during the 1940s and 1950s. Most of their products are relatively inexpensive. You can often buy an interesting piece for $10 to $50. Few examples cost more than $100 each.

EUROPEAN GLASS

Collectors are interested in European glass made during the 1940s and 1950s because it was sold, used and collected in the United States. However, examples are much more costly than American glass of the same period. Delicate handblown glass vases by the master Italian designer Venini cost $1,000 or more.

The most popular European glass was produced in the Scandinavian countries. Designers there were the first to introduce new, spectacular shapes. They also experimented with bright colors and unusual surface textures.

Some Scandinavian glass was mass-produced. Other examples were unique. You can purchase items by designers such as Gunnar Nylund and Berndt Friberg for as little as $50 or as much as $1,000.

Other interesting European glass was made in Italy, Germany and England.

Japan also produced some very appealing items. Some are similar to Scandinavian examples. This glass has been ignored by collectors. It can usually be purchased inexpensively.

Tumblers and juice glasses with brightly painted designs were found in most fashionable kitchens during the 1940s and 1950s. These examples cost $2 to $4 each.

COLLECTING 1940s AND 1950s GLASS

Items by popular manufacturers such as Heisey are available through most dealers.

Check Lesser-Known Factories—Many of these firms were small. Their wares were not widely distributed. Look for examples in the area in which the factory was located.

Visit Stores in Major Cities—Exotic foreign items such as Venini glass can be found in big-city shops specializing in memorabilia from the 1930s, 1940s and 1950s. Prices are high.

Study Different Types of Glass—Remember that many glass items were not marked. Others were marked with paper labels that have been lost. Familiarize yourself with different types of glass by reading books and catalogs. Visit the factories if you can. If you study the glass you want to collect, you will be able to recognize unmarked examples.

This is very important. You can often find glass items from this period at yard sales, church bazaars and secondhand-furniture stores. Few sellers know these items are collectible.

Consult Antique Dealers—Many dealers are not familiar with specific types of glass. Tell them about the types you are interested in. Ask them to contact you if they find such items.

Attend Estate Auctions—Most auction houses handle only Heisey or Depression glass. If you are interested in other types, attend estate auctions. Examples are often sold for moderate sums at such auctions.

Always check box lots or miscellaneous collections of kitchen or household objects. You may find one or more excellent glass items in an inexpensive box lot.

Join Collectors' Clubs—Enthusiasts are beginning to establish organizations for collectors of specific types of glass from this period. If there is a collectors' club associated with the items you want, join it! Selling, buying and swapping mementos with fellow enthusiasts is one of the best ways to add to your collection and increase your knowledge. You can make friends at the same time.

BUYING AND SELLING GLASS

• Few pieces were handmade during the 1940s and 1950s. Such pieces will bring premium prices in years to come. Look for examples of blown glass from shops such as the Pilgrim Glass Co. of West Virginia.

• Don't purchase damaged pieces. They have little value.

• Before you buy an item, check it carefully, preferably with a black light. This ultraviolet light will reveal any cracks or repairs.

• Look for fake manufacturers' marks. Some reproductions carry the names of defunct glass companies.

• Always check labels. Some unscrupulous sellers have copied early labels and attached them to unmarked pieces. An original label will be worn and faded.

Among the most spectacular examples of 1950s glass are the hand-blown handkerchief vases of Venini. Made about 1951, this important piece is worth $1,500 to $2,000. Similar pieces of lesser quality sell for several hundred dollars.

Collectibles showing TV puppet Howdy Doody and early Disney characters continue to grow in value and popularity. The 1950s Howdy juice glass costs $13 to $15. The affectionate tribute to Snow White's friend Dopey is an excellent value at $18.

METALWARE

Despite the development of plastics, many traditional materials were widely used during the 1940s and 1950s. These included various metals. Metalwares have been popular because of their strength and attractiveness. Today, many collectors are interested in stainless-steel, chrome, aluminum, brass, copper and pot-metal objects of the 1940s and 1950s.

CATEGORIES OF METALWARE

You can collect these objects by material, type or manufacturer.

Collecting by Material—If you collect this way, you will specialize in things made from one specific metal, such as chrome or copper.

Collecting by Type—If you use this technique, you will buy one kind of object, such as ashtrays or coffeepots, made of different metals.

You might also combine these two approaches and narrow your field. For example, you could purchase only chrome ashtrays or aluminum ice buckets.

Collecting by Manufacturer—Some enthusiasts acquire the products of one manufacturer. They buy the stainless-steel items made by the Ronson Corp. of Bridgewater, New Jersey, or the chrome objects made by the Manning Bowman Manufacturing Co. Some manufacturers already are popular with collectors. You might prefer purchasing items made by companies that are less well-known. Such mementos will be less expensive and more readily available.

Enthusiasts are most interested in objects made of chrome, aluminum, stainless steel, brass, copper and pot metal. A few collectors buy items made of iron or tin.

CHROME-PLATED STEEL

This is usually referred to as *chrome*. Utensils in this shiny, silvery metal are lightweight, durable and very attractive. Chrome objects were first produced in the 1930s in an Art Deco style.

The sleek, modern lines of these items have great appeal. Cocktail mixers resemble rocket ships and sugar bowls look like flying saucers.

The most popular chrome items are serving pieces. These include coffee and tea sets, including creamers

This brass and iron wall clock dates from the 1950s and is worth $65 to $100. It is typical of the spectacular starburst clocks of the period.

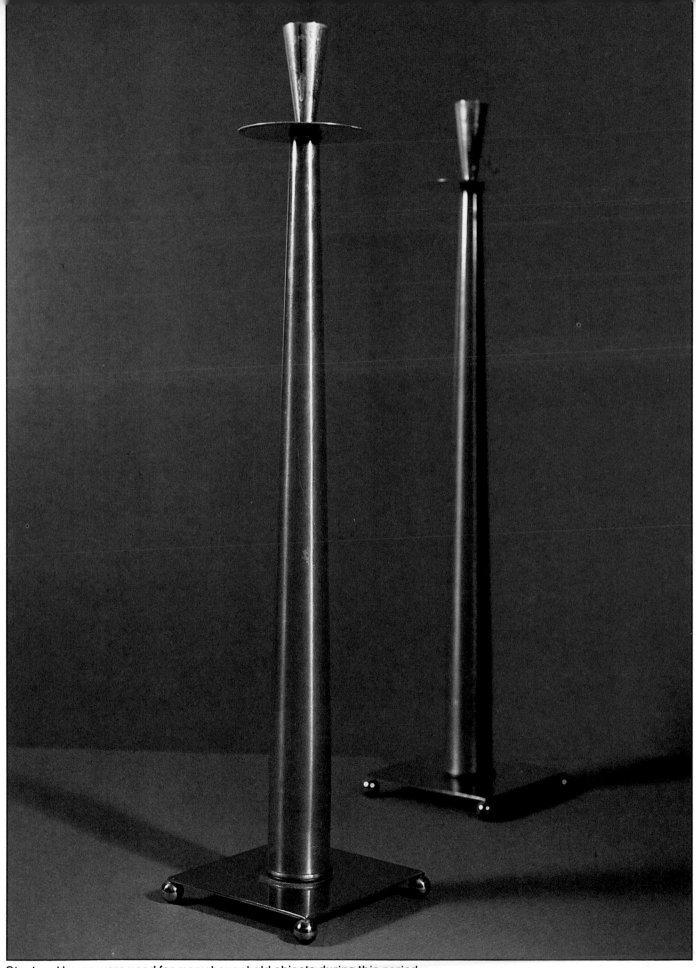

Steel and brass were used for many household objects during this period.
These materials were combined in this pair of geometric candlesticks, worth
$125 to $150.

and sugar bowls. Enthusiasts also collect serving trays, many of which folded for storage; cocktail mixers; goblets; ashtrays; cigarette boxes; lighters; bonbon trays; night lights and picture frames.

Many firms manufactured chrome-plated accessories, but the most popular products are those by the Chase Brass and Copper Co. of Waterbury, Connecticut and Cleveland, Ohio, and the Manning Bowman Manufacturing Co.

Chase Manufacturing Co.—This factory made metal objects with severe, simple shapes. There is intense competition among collectors of Chase products. As a result, marked waffle irons cost as much as $65, and cocktail shakers are $35 to $50.

Manning Bowman Manufacturing Co.—This firm often cleverly combined chrome with Bakelite, an early form of plastic.

If you want to pay less, look for unmarked items or examples by lesser-known manufacturers. Many reproductions are on the market, so be careful! Make sure you are getting an original.

ALUMINUM

Aluminum items are much less popular than chrome. They often cost a few dollars each. Ice buckets, trays, goblets, cocktail shakers, vanity cases and cigarette boxes are readily available. Many pieces of aluminum ware have a surface covered with a pattern of shallow indentations. This was created by a technique known as *hammering*. Similar patterns can be seen on late 19th-century silver. You can find marked aluminum, but most collectors don't think that manufacturers' marks are important.

STAINLESS STEEL

One of the great industrial materials used before World War II was stainless steel. It was more attractive than chrome or aluminum, but also more expensive. You will find attractive serving and eating utensils, cigarette cases, bookends and lighters.

The Ronson Corp.—This is the best-known manufacturer. It produced the famous Ronson lighters and humorous sculptural figures of horses, cats and dogs.

These poodle record holders date from the late 1940s and are made of iron wire. The smaller one, for 45s, is worth $75 to $125. The larger example holds 78s or LPs and costs $135 to $185.

Humorous novelties included cast-iron doorstops such as this parrot on a perch. It sells for $45 to $65.

Designed by Russell Wright, this aluminum, iron and wood punch set was made between 1945 and 1955. It costs $145 to $185. The set has 12 marked tumblers and an ice tray.

BRASS AND COPPER

These materials were not used extensively in the 1940s and 1950s. However, you can find desk lamps, serving dishes, umbrella stands, coffeepots and sculptural figures. Some of these figures are intended purely as "art." Others grace such household items as floor lamps and ashtrays.

Most brass and copper objects from this period were mass-produced. Many have very thin metal skins and are not well-made. Look for handcrafted objects. They have the greatest potential value.

POT METAL

Pot metal is a mixture of tin, lead and other metal alloys. It is pale silver and very lightweight. Items made with pot metal often resemble those made with more valuable materials. As a result, many manufacturers used pot metal during the 1940s and 1950s. They filled the core of their products with plaster or lead to make them as heavy as items made of more costly metals. Then they put a thin coat of finish over the objects, making them look like bronze, silver or gold.

If you are unsure what an item is made of, turn the piece upside down and check the base. Bronze, silver and other finishes quickly wear off in places, exposing the base metal. The pale-silver hue of the pot metal usually will show through.

Many 1940s and 1950s collectibles were made of pot metal. They included many floor and table lamps, doorstops, banks, statuettes, ashtrays and thermometers. These objects are easy to find and inexpensive. Pot-metal items are ideal acquisitions if you want a large collection and have plenty of room.

IRON AND TIN

Iron fireplace tools and tin cooking utensils are readily available. However, few collectors purchase these objects.

The U.S. government used iron and tin to make war materials from 1941 to 1945. Manufacturers could not use these metals for other items during those years.

COLLECTING METALWARE

Metalware is available from numerous sources.

Check Antique Shops—Many enthusiasts are buying chrome and stainless-steel items. These are expensive. You can find such pieces in some antique shops, especially in larger cities.

Attend Auctions—You can sometimes locate good examples at small estate or country auctions. They are usually offered as household goods. You will seldom find metalware from the 1940s and 1950s at auctions.

Go to Secondhand Stores—You may find the best bargains at secondhand stores, yard sales and charity bazaars. Many people don't realize metal items are valuable.

Have Wiring Checked—If you buy electrical appliances such as lamps or chrome-plated waffle irons, be sure to have the wiring checked by an electrician before you use them. Most old electrical appliances need repairs before they can be used safely.

BUYING AND SELLING METALWARE

- Chrome-plated steel items are the most popular. Prices are increasing. Look for Chase and Manning Bowman products.
- Collect aluminum wares. These items are interesting and much less expensive than chrome-plated steel pieces.
- The most popular pot-metal pieces are the nymph-like Art Deco figures. They are covered with a bronze or green stain to resemble items made of more costly metals. These small statuettes are charming novelties. Some are combined with a lamp or clock.
- Before you buy an item, check the base to make sure you know what metal it is made of.

Chrome items were popular during this time and are excellent bargains. This chrome cocktail mixer costs $15 to $20. It was made between 1955 and 1960.

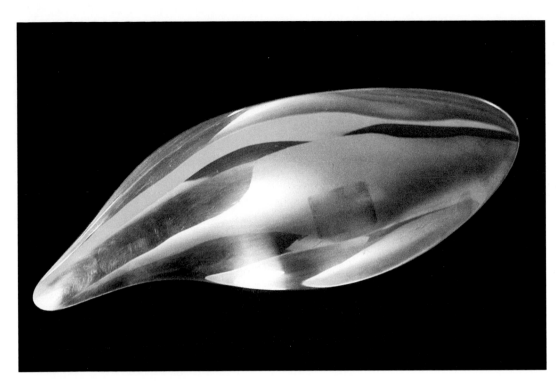

Designed for the firm Reed and Barton by the famous sculptor Alexander Calder, this silver nut dish costs $85 to $135. It was made between 1955 and 1960.

Made of brass and anodized steel, this Italian table lamp has the sleek lines and ultramodern look that distinguished many European items made during this era. Such pieces cost $300 to $400. Demand for these items is increasing.

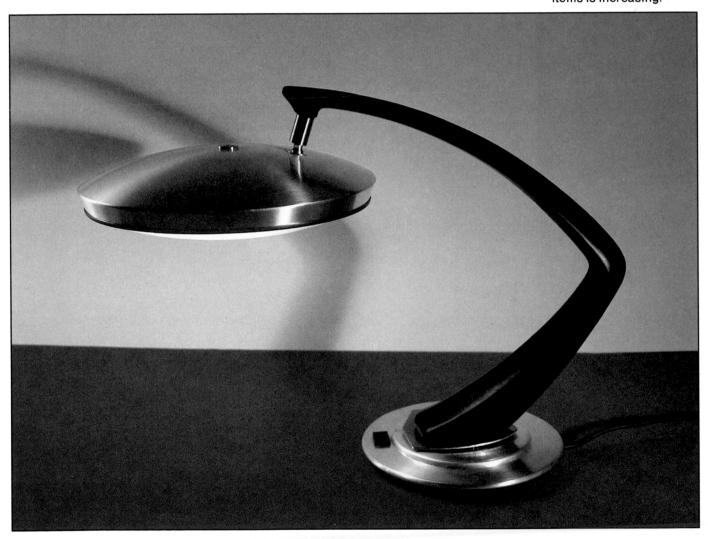

PLASTICS

Plastics were developed long before 1940. The earliest well-known example was Bakelite, made in 1907 by Belgian-born chemist Leo Baekeland. However, these materials did not become widely used until World War II.

Most people think of plastics as synthetic materials made from oil and coal tars. However, some plastics are made from latex or horn. Anything that can be softened by heat and molded into a permanent shape qualifies as a plastic. Today, collectors can find hundreds of interesting, colorful objects made of plastic.

CATEGORIES OF PLASTICS

You can collect plastics several different ways.

Collecting by Type—You can collect one type of object, such as kitchen or household tools. Many disposable knives, forks, spoons and napkin rings were made of plastic during the 1940s and 1950s.

Powder boxes and other dressing-table accessories are also popular.

Other collectibles include clocks, phonographs, phonograph records, hair dryers, automobile dashboards, wastebaskets and "tortoise-shell" combs, which were really plastic.

Cigarette boxes made during the 1950s are especially attractive. They feature embossed designs, including sporting scenes, abstract compositions and floral patterns.

One reason these items are popular is their style. They come in bright hues and interesting shapes. Another reason is that they are very inexpensive.

Collecting by Manufacturer—Many enthusiasts concentrate on acquiring objects made by one factory.

Collecting by Material—You can also collect items made of one type of plastic. Bakelite objects are already popular and difficult to find, especially the exotic radios made between 1930 and 1950.

Other Categories—Another way to limit your collection is to buy plastic items that fall within a recognized collecting category. For example, you might decide to collect advertising items—called *advertiques.* You could concentrate on buying only plastic examples. Such items include an Oscar Mayer hot dog, $5 to $7; a plastic beer-foam scraper, $5 to $15; or the hard plastic knobs used on beer kegs. Dozens of plastic advertiques are available.

This 1950s table lamp is plastic combined with stainless and enameled steel. It costs $85 to $135.

The streamlined look of the 1950s could be seen in the most unlikely products. This plastic and steel fan, the Air-Flight by W. W. Welch, is a functioning museum piece. It costs $125 to $175.

Plastic was sometimes combined with other materials. These plastic and woven-paper coasters from the early 1950s are worth $12 to $17.

This plastic two-piece storage container shaped like a woman is worth
about $35 to $55. It was produced between 1945 and 1955.

Another interesting category involves *look-alikes*. Plastics can resemble many materials, including wood, glass, metal, even silk or wool. You could assemble a houseful of plastic objects that look like wool drapes, metal statues or wood furniture.

COLLECTING PLASTICS

Collectors are becoming increasingly interested in plastic items made during the 1940s and 1950s. Now is the time to decide what you want to collect and to start looking for it. You should be able to acquire many items at very low prices.

Talk with Dealers—Finding what you want may require some work. A few dealers in larger cities stock plastic radios, jewelry and furniture. Most antique and memorabilia shops don't carry such items.

Check Storage Areas—Look in attics, basements, barns, lofts and crawl spaces. Visit stores going out of business, secondhand shops, flea markets and yard sales. Most plastic items are considered junk. Prices are low. You should be able to buy many items for a few dollars or even a few cents.

Don't Purchase Damaged Items—Buy only items in good condition. Almost all plastic objects were mass-produced in great quantities. If you are willing to wait, you will find what you want.

Learn About the Field—Few books or magazines deal with plastic items. Most references deal only with radios or are too general to be useful. You have the opportunity to contribute new information to this area. It is a rare opportunity. Form collectors' clubs and produce newsletters to publicize what you learn. Plastics collectors are pioneers!

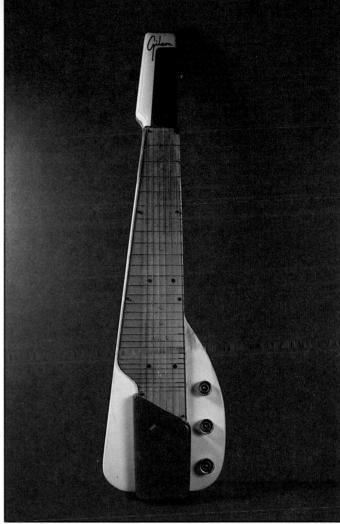

You could play this 1950s plastic and metal guitar by Gibson, but most collectors would hang it on the wall. It is worth $125 to $175.

BUYING AND SELLING PLASTICS

- Most plastic items are very inexpensive. However, prices are increasing.
- Buy dishware and knickknacks now. Within a few years, these items will be much more valuable.
- Don't buy worn or damaged pieces. Plastic items are readily available, so you can be choosy.
- Buy pieces showing little or no wear. Such pieces are referred to as being in *mint condition*.
- Save any boxes or instructional materials that come with a plastic item. As with all collectibles, the *go-withs* accompanying plastic mementos enhance the value of these pieces.

This plastic and wrought-iron planter is $20 to $25. The bullet shape seen here was used in many items made during the 1950s, including electric mixers and automobiles.

HOUSEHOLD COLLECTIBLES

The objects that our parents used around the house bring back memories. These nostalgic feelings are the main reasons collectors are buying household items of the 1940s and 1950s.

It is easy to recall the ordinary objects we grew up with. These items include the boxes, jars and tins that food, beauty aids and laundry soap came in. They also include the clocks that prodded us off to school and the napkin rings and potholders that awaited us when we came home for dinner. All were so commonplace that hardly anyone thought about them. All are collectible today.

Thousands of these objects are available. They were made of many different materials, including metal, plastic, wood and plaster.

CATEGORIES OF HOUSEHOLD COLLECTIBLES

The field of 1940s and 1950s household collectibles is very broad. You will probably want to focus on one limited category. Such categories include creating an environment, black memorabilia, containers and utensils.

Creating an Environment—Some collectors interested in this field create an environment. They install a fine old chrome-and-enamel gas range of the 1940s in their kitchen. They surround it with usable artifacts. These might include several Griswold cast-iron frying pans and muffin molds, a few boxes of Gold Dust Twins soap powder, and Aunt Jemima pancake mix.

Black Memorabilia—Some enthusiasts collect black memorabilia. Many of these items are deplorable reminders of racial stereotypes. They include scrub brushes and wood towel racks topped with carved representations of smiling black women. Ceramic and plastic salt and pepper shakers were often shaped like black couples or children.

Black memorabilia is so varied that some dealers specialize in it. Prices are rising. A character umbrella, ashtray or dustpan that sold for a few dollars five years ago now costs $30 to $50.

Plaster-cast wall decorations were very popular. This example, by John Douglas, costs $125 to $175. It has the realism and detail beloved by advanced collectors.

Even wastebaskets are collectible! This iron-wire, canvas and plastic suspension-type example was manufactured between 1950 and 1960. It costs $35 to $45.

The comic-strip characters Jiggs holds a 1940s ashtray. This piece, made of carved, painted wood, is worth $75 to $125.

Advertising symbols were used on many household items during the 1940s and 1950s. This glass and plastic Nestea dispenser was designed to hold iced tea. It costs $90 to $130.

Food and Utility Containers—Manufacturers have long recognized that advertising is good business. A snappy slogan, good graphics and bright colors attract customers. Some of the most interesting food, soap-powder and beauty-aid containers were produced during the 1940s and 1950s.

Look for talcum-powder tins, lithographed-tin cookie and candy boxes, and round metal cracker boxes.

Large, molded-glass Planters Peanuts jars are collectible. Enthusiasts are also purchasing bottles and jars used for preserving food.

The most valuable objects are those that are colorful or closely associated with a movie star, singer or other glamorous sponsor.

Household Utensils—Collectibles include textiles, such as potholders, napkins, tablecloths and bedspreads.

Wood kitchenwares include towel racks, napkin holders, brushes, spice racks, small cabinets, Lazy Susans, even unusual mops or brooms.

Metals objects include sets of brightly painted tin canisters, dustpans, picture frames, ashtrays, match holders and cooking utensils.

Rarer items include desk sets, cigarette and cigar boxes, handkerchief and jewelry boxes, and wall thermometers. Electric and windup clocks of the period are very interesting mementos.

Clocks made of chrome combined with Bakelite, other plastic or tinted glass are especially popular. Chrome and blue-glass desk or dresser clocks produced during the 1940s also interest collectors, primarily because of the sleek Art Deco styling. You can also find clocks in pot metal, imitation tortoise shell, stainless steel or wood. Well-known manufacturers include The Ansonia Clock Co. of Brooklyn, New York, Waterbury Clock Co. of Waterbury, Connecticut, and the Hammond Clock Co. of Chicago. Ronson made wonderful devices that combined clocks and cigarette lighters.

COLLECTING HOUSEHOLD ITEMS

Dealers carry some period clocks. However, you will find most household items made during the 1940s and 1950s in attics, basements and secondhand shops.

This whimsical soft-drink poster from the 1940s is highly prized by collectors. It is worth $50 to $65.

Pillows such as this patriotic example from the 1940s were popular gifts. They are worth $15 to $25 each.

Attend Auctions—These sales can be good sources, especially estate auctions in small communities. Most items will be sold as used household goods. Be sure to check box lots. Choice examples of kitchen and household accessories are dumped into these lots by people who assume such items have little value.

Durable household or kitchen accessories such as iron pots and wood wall racks are still being used. You can sometimes find excellent bargains by advertising in local newspapers.

Check with Neighbors—People often throw out old items when cleaning basements or attics.

Ask Demolition Companies—These firms are good sources for items made during the 1940s and 1950s. In large cities such as New York, collectors have found everything from salvageable enamel-top gas stoves to interesting medicine cabinets at demolition companies.

Consult Experts—Remember to have an expert thoroughly check any old electrical or gas-powered appliances before you use them.

BUYING AND SELLING HOUSEHOLD COLLECTIBLES

- Items with advertising, such as soap-powder and food containers, are fun to collect.
- Avoid damaged or water-stained mementos.
- Watch out for reproductions. Some popular advertiques, or advertising collectibles, are being reproduced.
- Items associated with black memorabilia are becoming popular and expensive. Beginning collectors should avoid these.
- Purchase one type of memento. Interesting small collections can range from embroidered potholders to Bakelite napkin holders.

This chrome, glass and vinyl traveling vanity mirror was made during the 1950s. Small household items such as this are readily available at yard sales and flea markets. This piece is worth $80 to $110. Its value is increasing steadily.

Never discard textiles made during this period. Dressmakers and furniture upholsterers use them. Collectors are also becoming interested in these fabrics. These patterns cost $3 to $5 per yard. They were produced in the 1950s.

MOVIE, RADIO AND TELEVISION MEMORABILIA

The 1940s and 1950s were an entertainer's paradise. Wartime restrictions on themes and materials were lifted. The movie industry boomed. The number of radio stations increased. Television became a national craze.

Hundreds of items associated with the entertainment industry during this period are collectible. These include posters, autographs and premiums. If you are interested in this area, you must limit your options.

Collecting by Celebrity—You might want to specialize in items relating to a single celebrity. The most popular stars collected today include John Wayne, James Dean and Ronald Reagan. Remember that objects relating to obscure performers were made in smaller quantities and may become more valuable than items relating to more well-known personalities.

Collecting by Type of Memento—You might collect one type of item. You could acquire only radio premiums or movie posters.

Creating a Category—You could design your own category. This might involve posters relating to movies about World War II or autographs of television comedians.

You can approach collecting in many ways. Remember that if you choose a category that is too broad, you will have problems assembling a representative collection. If you select an area that is too narrow, you will have difficulty finding acquisitions.

Most items are inexpensive. For example, hundreds of stars' autographs are available for $1 to $3 each. Many movie and television props and radio premiums cost less than $20 each.

However, some items are very expensive. A signed picture of James Dean may cost $1,000. The sled *Rosebud*, featured in the famous movie *Citizen Kane*, brought more than $60,000 at auction. Collect what you like, but be sure you can afford it!

Movie, radio and television collectibles include posters, premiums, promotional items, paper dolls, books, stills and films.

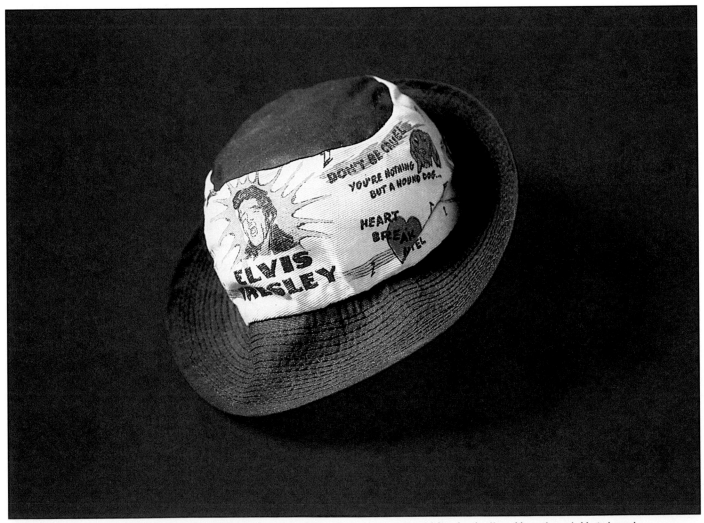

This Elvis Presley fan's hat has the names of some of the singer's greatest hits, including *Heartbreak Hotel* and *You Ain't Nuthin' But a Hound Dog.* This item is a bargain at $25 to $35. It will increase in value.

This picture of Elvis Presley is a popular collectible. Unsigned, it is worth $30 to $40. An authentic autograph would increase the price to $300 or $400.

POSTERS

Perhaps the most popular movie collectible is the poster. More than 200 million were produced during the past 50 years. Because thousands of examples from the 1940s and 1950s are available, prices are reasonable. You can buy a poster from the Mickey Rooney movie *Andy Hardy Comes Home* for $9 to $13. Posters for films such as *Abbott & Costello Meet the Invisible Man* sell for $15 to $25. However, some items are costly. A poster from *Easter Parade,* with Judy Garland and Fred Astaire, brings $350 to $400. A few posters cost more than $1,000 each.

Collectors usually categorize posters according to size and content.

One Sheets—These are the large, 27 x 41-inch illustrations placed outside the movie house.

Inserts—These items measure 14 by 36 inches and show details of the film. They are placed in the lobby.

Lobby Cards—These posters are 11 by 14 inches and come in sets of eight. They begin with a title card and show dramatic scenes from the film.

Most posters show signs of wear, including tack holes. This is usually not a serious problem. However, don't buy examples that are torn or badly stained. Such posters are worth 30% to 60% less than undamaged ones.

RADIO PREMIUMS

Radio premiums, or *giveaways,* were usually made for children. Some premiums were products promoted on a radio program. Others were prizes that listeners could get by sending in a boxtop or label from the product along with a few cents to cover postage.

Examples include the Howdy Doody Ovaltine mug, the Roy Rogers signet ring and membership buttons for the Captain Marvel fan club. These pieces are very popular with collectors. Prices remain moderate because so many examples were made. Most of these items cost $10 to $45 each.

MISCELLANEOUS PROMOTIONAL ITEMS

These items were usually sold rather than given away. Many of these mementos featured radio, television and movie characters.

Popular collectibles include the Bambi salt and pepper set and the Donald Duck ashtray. Enthusiasts also like metal or plastic lunchboxes and thermos jugs featuring cartoon and television characters. Examples include Lassie, Batman, the Flintstones and the Roadrunner. Most of these items cost $5 to $15 each.

PAPER DOLLS

Another popular category comprises paper dolls. Male stars such as Rock Hudson can be found, but the majority featured the "love goddesses" of the 1940s and 1950s. The popularity of these women has not declined. Prices are high. A Bette Davis set sells for $55 to $70. Lana Turner costs $30 to $40, and Grace Kelly is $90 to $115.

Don't cut up an uncut sheet! Original uncut sheets of paper dolls are worth two to three times as much as individual figures and costumes.

BOOKS

Books, pamphlets and other *ephemera,* or paper goods, related to movies, television and radio are interesting and inexpensive.

Children's Books—Coloring or paint books featuring movie stars or cartoon characters are easy to find.

Other children's books include the *Big Little Books,* with Andy Panda, Mickey Mouse and Howdy Doody.

Pop-up books—These are also popular. They have colorful paper figures that "pop-up" when the book is opened.

Press Books—Collectors interested in history buy press books. These provided promotional material about movies. Some included sheet music of songs from the films. Some press books are more expensive because they are more difficult to find. The press book for *Destination Tokyo,* with Cary Grant, is $40 to $50. Press books that are not as rare are much less costly. The press book for Bing Crosby's *White Christmas* is $5 to $8.

Sheet Music—Because few enthusiasts collect it, sheet music is an excellent bargain. You can purchase an illustrated version of *Moonlight Becomes You,* from *The Road to Morocco* with Bob Hope and Bing Crosby, for $2 to $4. Judy Garland's version of the *Trolley Song* from *Meet Me in St. Louis* costs $5 to $8.

STILLS AND FILMS

Stills are glossy pictures of celebrities or movie scenes. They were produced in great quantities. Such photos were used for publicity and sold to fans. They are extremely inexpensive. Most cost $1 to $2. Many autographed stills of less-popular stars are $2 to $5.

Autographed material relating to major celebrities is more expensive. An autographed picture of Elizabeth Taylor is $15 to $25. A similar example of Marilyn Monroe costs $175 to $225.

Many collectors buy stills of lesser-known actors and actresses, hoping that future television revivals or other events will make these people more popular. This can happen. Look at Ronald Reagan.

Collectors show increasing interest in 8mm and 16mm films. This field is expensive. Most films cost $100 to $250. However, many serious film buffs enjoy owning copies of such hits as *Night of the Living Dead* and *Beach Blanket Bingo.*

TELEVISION MEMORABILIA

If you decide to buy television collectibles, you will have hundreds of items to choose from. These include puzzles, postcards, pencil boxes, comic books, even a Davy Crockett wall light.

The Mickey Mouse Club provided a tray to fans who wanted to eat dinner while watching the program. Hopalong Cassidy offered a milk mug, and Superman an identification card. Even the weekly *TV Guide* is collectible. Early issues cost as much as $60 each!

COLLECTING MOVIE, RADIO AND TELEVISION MEMORABILIA

You can find movie, radio and TV memorabilia in many places.

Ask Dealers—Some dealers specialize in this area. A few operate mail-order businesses, so you can buy and sell by mail.

Check Advertisements—Look through the ads in the publications of such groups as the Motion Pictures Collectibles Association. Joining one of these collectors' groups might also be worthwhile.

Attend Auctions—Memorabilia auctions sometimes include interesting items. The estates of show-business people often provide excellent mementos.

Yard sales and church bazaars seldom have this type of memorabilia. These items have attracted collec-

tors' attention only within the past decade. Few early collections exist.

Visit Theaters—Old movie houses, radio stations, newsstands and bookstores can be very good sources of memorabilia.

Place Your Own Ads—You can often find magazines, premiums and books this way. Be sure your ad clearly describes the items you are looking for.

Beware of Forgeries—Fakes and reproductions are not a major problem in this field, but watch out for forged autographs of major stars such as James Dean. Many Marilyn Monroe items have also been reproduced.

BUYING AND SELLING MOVIE, RADIO AND TELEVISION MEMORABILIA

● Enthusiasts have collected these items for years. Rare autographs, movie posters and personal memorabilia of the stars cost thousands of dollars.
● If you don't want to spend that much, buy radio premiums or paper dolls.
● Books, magazines and sheet music associated with movies or television and radio programs are popular, inexpensive mementos.
● Build a collection around one or two stars. Such a collection will have depth and variety. It will be more interesting and valuable than a collection that includes a few items from many stars.

Fanzines and movie magazines from the 1940s and 1950s will grow in value. The movie star decals are worth more in their original packaging. These magazines are worth $7 to $10 each; the decals $2 to $3 each.

JEWELRY

Many 1940s and 1950s enthusiasts collect the jewelry and clothing of this period. Movie stars and early television personalities are remembered not only for who they were, but what they wore. Rhinestone bracelets and plastic pearls were popularized by Betty Grable. The gaudy Hawaiian shirt was Howdy Doody's trademark. These figures sparked a stylistic revolution. Collectors today buy these items to preserve or to wear.

CATEGORIES OF JEWELRY

If you are a jewelry collector of modest means, the baubles of the 1940s and 1950s are an excellent buy. Jewelry of this era varies greatly in appearance and material. Some pieces were made with traditional precious metals and gems. But many more rings, bracelets and necklaces were made with inexpensive materials such as wood, glass, pot metal and plastic.

The war years were a period of conservative style and dress. It did not seem right to be wearing flashy jewelry while so many people were fighting overseas. But after the soldiers returned, designers became more innovative. Most people did not have very much money, so bright, inexpensive styles were in vogue. Costume jewelry became a national fad. Its sharp lines and geometric shapes were reminiscent of Art Deco.

Designers used various materials for this jewelry.

Plastic—One of the most popular materials was plastic, especially Bakelite. Bright orange, green, red, yellow and blue Bakelite jewelry sold for $1 to $2 in the 1940s. Today, you will pay $15 to $45. Collectors are especially interested in bracelets, rings, brooches, pins and hair clips.

Plastic was also used in the character pins popular in the 1950s. Mickey Mouse, Donald Duck, Goofy and other Disney characters are featured on this jewelry.

Wood—Saw-cut and painted wood pins and earrings were also popular during this time. Large earrings shaped like butterflies and birds sprouted from the ears of maids and matrons. These bangles now cost $5 to $10 a pair.

Pot Metal and Glass—These materials were often combined to create—more or less—the appearance of diamond and silver finery. Most such pieces were done in traditional Victorian styles. However, some baubles were more flamboyant. The flashy earrings, large finger rings and long necklaces made during this time are what most of us associate with the term *costume jewelry.*

Sterling Silver and Enamel—Some Art Deco examples of pot-metal and glass jewelry are available. However, many of the finest pieces were produced from more costly materials. Sophisticated collectors look for the fine geometric necklaces, pendants, earrings and bracelets made of sterling silver and enamel. Enameled silver jewelry is much in demand. Even small pieces cost $50 to $175.

Other Materials—The more naturalistic brooches, rings and bracelets introduced after World War II by the well-known designer George Jensen are also popular. He usually worked in silver. Prices start at $100.

Many designers and manufacturers also produced charms. These small figures of animals, people, cars, shoes and dozens of other objects were hung from a bracelet worn about the wrist or ankle. Charm bracelets were one of the fashion rages of the 1950s, and many can be found today. Pot-metal charms cost $2 to $3 each. Silver charms are $3 to $10. Prices are rising. The charm-bracelet fad, like so many other 1950s trends, has returned.

COLLECTING JEWELRY

Jewelry is usually collected to be worn. Collect what you like! Remember that most of these items were mass-produced and are easy to find.

Check Dealers and Sales—Many dealers stock these baubles. You can also find them at yard sales and charity bazaars. Sellers usually assume that the only pieces of value are those made of gold, silver or precious stones.

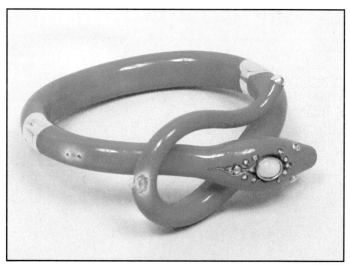

Unusual jewelry was a fad in the 1950s. This spectacular snake-form bracelet is banded in gold and now worth between $150 and $200.

This elaborate glass and metal choker was designed by Miriam Haskell, one of the most important names in 1950s costume jewelry. It is valued at $135 to $165. The plastic display hand is worth $35 to $55.

Visit Flea Markets—One of the best ways to add to your collection is to dig through the boxes of costume jewelry at these markets.

Go to Auctions—Better-quality examples such as those by Jensen are offered at auctions specializing in 1940s and 1950s memorabilia. You might also find interesting items at estate auctions.

Buy Jewelry in Good Condition—Don't purchase damaged pieces. Broken jewelry or pieces with missing elements are very difficult and costly to repair. Only the rarest or most desirable specimens are worth the time and expense. Most of the time, you would be wiser to wait until you find a similar piece in better condition.

BUYING AND SELLING
JEWELRY AND CLOTHING

- Costume jewelry is a good field. Bakelite character pins and pieces mounted in silver are especially popular.
- Pot-metal pieces are bargains.
- Make sure pieces are complete. Earrings and necklaces often had bangles, which may have been lost. Compare all pieces in a set to be sure they match.
- Clothing from the 1940s and 1950s is fashionable today. Beware of reproductions. Hawaiian shirts and Marilyn Monroe gowns are widely copied.
- An original Howdy Doody shirt is an excellent buy.
- Check secondhand stores and yard sales. They offer many reasonably priced items.

Small, wearable objects, such as brooches and unusual buttons, made of Bakelite, Catalin and other plastics are much in demand. These charming pins are $8 each.

These rhinestone, plastic and gilded-metal bracelets are becoming popular again. The expansion-band bracelets cost $60 to $75 each. The plastic and rhinestone examples are $25 to $40.

CLOTHING

If you want to collect the clothes of the 1940s and 1950s, you are in luck. These items are readily available, usually at modest prices.

CATEGORIES OF CLOTHING

Clothing from this era is again fashionable. Young people, rock stars, and movie and TV personalities are wearing shirts, suits and shoes from this period. You can dress yourself in the slinky synthetic gowns that Marilyn Monroe favored, or sport a pair of the pointy-toed alligator shoes that George Raft liked so much.

Hats—Almost everything from this period is collectible. Hats are especially popular. Women are looking for the large feathered hats that set off fashionably long hair. Men want the tough-looking snap brims from Dobson and Stetson.

Dresses and Gowns—These items, especially those made of synthetics such as rayon, are collected by many young women. The colors are bold and the styles evoke prom-night nostalgia.

Many gowns worn in movies were later mass-produced. You could buy a gown similar to the one worn by Marilyn Monroe in *Some Like It Hot.*

Shoes—Women are also purchasing the elevated spike heels of the 1950s. Many originals are still available.

Men's shoes are less distinctive because styles change more slowly. Two types—alligator and suede—are characteristic of the era.

Suits and Jackets—If you ever wanted a zoot suit and were frustrated by parental opposition, now is the time to buy one. Don't forget the long brass or gold-plated key chain!

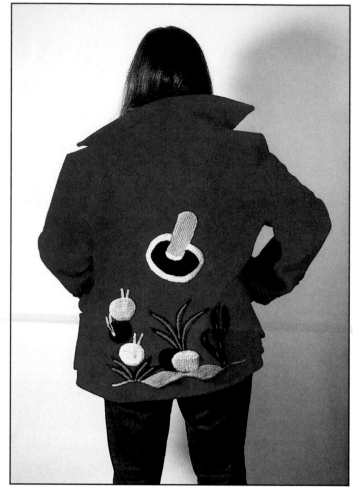

Clothing during the 1950s was big and bold. This red felt jacket is a bargain at $35 to $55. Its value will increase.

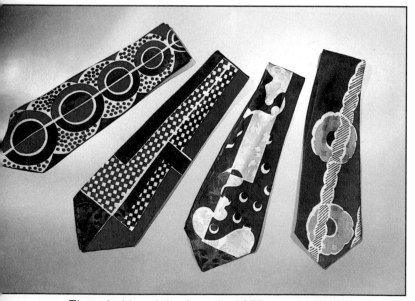

These bold neckties from the 1950s are made from silk. Some are handpainted. They cost from $8 to $12 each.

Patterned men's bathing trunks of the 1940s and early 1950s also have a tropical motif. The are modestly priced at $10 to $20.

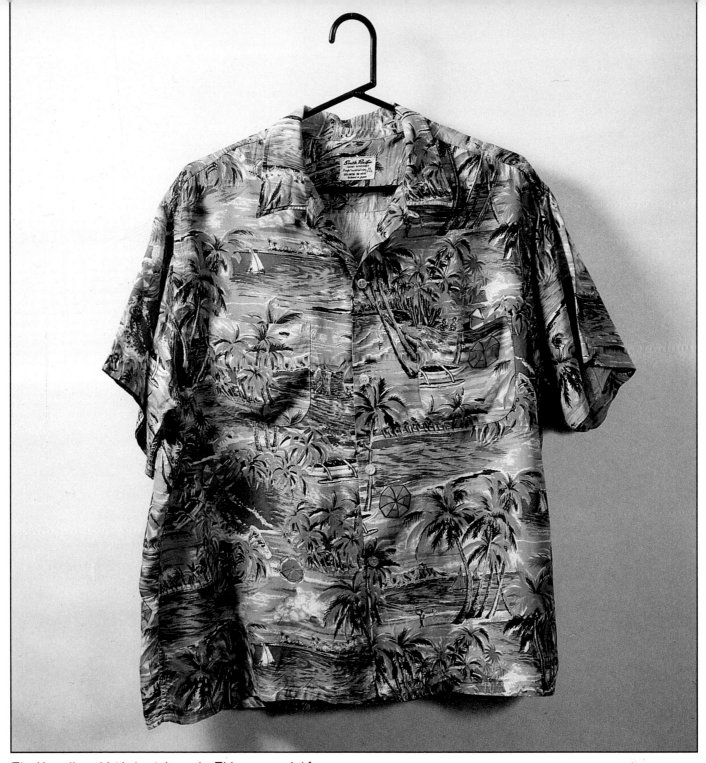

The Hawaiian shirt is in style again. This rayon print from the late 1950s costs $75 to $90. Earlier shirts in cotton are worth several hundred dollars each.

Furs—These items were synonymous with the times. Many women bought seal jackets or full-length minks. With the return to luxury in the 1980s, furs are in fashion again. Antique furs are a bargain. You can often buy an older fur in good condition for one-tenth the cost of a contemporary piece. Condition is very important. Moths and dampness can ruin older furs. Check any prospective purchase thoroughly.

Shirts and Blouses—These are necessities for a total 1940s or 1950s look. The Hawaiian shirt is all the rage now. A period piece can be valuable. Floppy rock-'n-roll shirts favored by jitterbugs are also popular. Remember, the brighter the better. Taste and moderation have no place here. These items were widely copied, so beware of imitations.

Accessories—Purses, gloves and patterned socks interest ambitious collectors. Ties are also popular—even the big wide ones with the battery-charged light that said, "Kiss me in the dark, baby"!

If they wore it, you want it.

COLLECTING CLOTHING

Clothing from this era is easy to find.

Check Dealers—Many antique and collectibles dealers stock clothing. However, they sometimes charge high prices.

Visit Secondhand Stores—You can find clothing at much lower prices in Salvation Army stores and other secondhand shops.

Go to Yard Sales—Many items from this period were stored away when outgrown or out of style. You can often find period pieces at yard sales. They usually have just emerged from an attic or storeroom.

Don't Purchase Damaged Clothing—Because so many items are available, you can be choosy. Only buy pieces in good condition. Restoration is time-consuming and can be expensive.

Avoid cracked leather and cloth that is thin or torn. Lightly soiled clothing can be cleaned, but dark stains usually won't come out.

Don't Purchase Incomplete Outfits—Don't buy pants without jackets or dresses without belts. You will find complete examples if you are patient.

Printed cotton skirts such as this 1950s example cost $25 to $45.

Alligator shoes were a sign of distinction for women and men. This spectacular pair of platform pumps is worth $55 to $85.

Building a Collection

If you decide to collect 1940s and 1950s memorabilia, you will have a distinct advantage. Unlike collectors of vintage toys or silver, you don't have to look long and hard for what you want. You are surrounded by collectibles.

ADVANTAGES FOR COLLECTORS

Many items are inexpensive. There are good reasons for this. Collectibles from this era are not very old. Many are still being used. Others have only recently been stored away or consigned to a secondhand shop.

In addition, many of these mementos were mass-produced. Chairs and tables were made by the thousands. Tableware and novelty items were manufactured by the millions.

These factors assure collectors of an abundant supply at low prices. A piece of rare designer furniture may cost thousands of dollars. A one-of-a-kind Marilyn Monroe poster may cost even more. However, these items are the exceptions. Most mementos from the 1940s and 1950s are very inexpensive!

DECIDING WHAT TO COLLECT

Faced with such a wide range of affordable items, you may ask, "What shall I collect?" Your answer should be based on personal taste. This book provides some guidelines for making your decision.

Buy Items You Can Use—Remember that unlike older and more expensive collectibles, 1940s and 1950s objects can be used as well as collected. Enthusiasts are decorating their homes with furniture by designers such as Eames. They are eating off tableware by Russell Wright and shaking their drinks in Chase cocktail shakers.

If something breaks, it can be replaced. If you are interested in nostalgia, think about decorating a kitchen, living room or your entire house with items made during the 1940s and 1950s. You would probably spend less than if you bought comparable contemporary furnishings.

Buy Practical, Attractive Mementos—If you decide to collect on a more limited scale, choose a field that is practical and pleasing to you. If you live in a small house, acquiring movie memorabilia may be more sensible than buying period furniture. If you have children or pets, buying plastics may be preferable to purchasing glassware.

Buy Items You Can Afford—Don't be intimidated by the number of available items. You don't have to collect everything! Buy what you like, can afford and can display properly. The following suggestions can help you get started.

COLLECTING BY CATEGORY

As with all antiques and collectibles, those from the 1940s and 1950s can be categorized several ways.

Collecting by Type—One way to categorize items is to classify them by type or function. Furniture, jewelry and books are types of objects.

However, you need to narrow your selection further. You can do this by collecting one type of item made of one kind of material. For example, you could buy only plastic earrings or books dealing with Westerns filmed during the 1940s.

Collecting by Manufacturer—You can also categorize collectibles according to their manufacturers. Most items made during the 1940s and 1950s have manufacturers' marks. Instead of trying to acquire every chrome accessory made during this time—an impossible task—you could purchase only those bearing the mark of the Chase Brass and Copper Co.

Adjusting Your Category—Choosing a category is a personal matter. Remember that you can adjust your category as you become more knowledgeable. You may start out collecting one type of item and decide this is too limiting. Or you may discover your original category is too broad, and needs to be restricted.

As you adjust your category, you will probably want to sell or trade some items. This book will provide tips on doing this most effectively.

Remember that dented, cracked, chipped or otherwise damaged pieces such the ones shown here have little value. Don't buy an extensively damaged piece unless it is extremely rare and valuable.

Many lamps and other electrical appliances have badly frayed or poorly repaired cords. Don't use such items until they have been checked by an electrician.

The most important thing to remember is that your collection should reflect your interests. Choose a category that includes items you can afford and can display appropriately. Don't let collecting categories become straitjackets that limit the pleasure you get from your hobby.

COLLECTING BY PERIOD

In many areas of collecting, age affects the value of an item. Collectors usually start by purchasing newer, less-expensive objects and buy older, more costly items later. A silver collector's first acquisitions might be 20th-century items made of electroplated silver. Later purchases might include objects made of 18th-century sterling silver.

However, the situation is different with 1940s and 1950s memorabilia. Because these items were made within a very narrow time span, age is not usually a significant factor in determining value. Rarity is usually much more important. An item made in limited quantities will usually be worth more than a similar memento that is 10 or 15 years older but more readily available.

There are exceptions. For example, a popular piece of furniture may have been produced for 30 or 40 years. Earlier examples may be worth much more to knowledgeable collectors who are aware of slight design changes made during that time.

The famous Cesca side chair by Marcel Breuer was first made in 1928. Examples produced in the 1950s look superficially like the earlier ones. However, the materials, screw placements and angle of the chair back are different. Such differences are not insignificant. A 1930s Cesca chair is worth several thousand dollars. A similar chair made in 1955 is worth several hundred.

Even though you may not want to concentrate on the earliest designs of this era, you should be familiar with them. Recognizing a rare, early piece could result in an economic windfall.

Textiles from the 1940s and 1950s can be used for wall hangings and furniture coverings. Notice how fresh and clean this bolt of 40-year-old fabric is.

Back-lighted glass shelves provide an interesting environment for your collection. Display your memorabilia in a way that pleases you.

COLLECTING BY DESIGNER

As you read this book, certain names reappear: Charles Eames, Gilbert Rohde, Russell Wright. These designers created some of the most beautiful mementos of the 1940s and 1950s. Advanced collectors are buying their work.

Collecting by designer can be interesting and profitable. If you can afford to buy pieces by Eames or Rohde, your acquisitions may become quite valuable. Because these pieces are already popular, they are costly. If you are a beginning collector with a limited budget, you are better off buying less-expensive, production-line items.

LIMITING YOUR COLLECTION

This book discusses only a few of the possible collecting categories. You will think of others, and you will meet collectors who have taken unique approaches. The important thing is to find a category that suits your circumstances and desires. Experience shows that you will get the best results by following several basic rules.

Choose a Category Carefully—The ideal collecting category lets you expand your collection in a reasonable, orderly manner. It should not be so broad that you run out of money or space. It should not be so narrow that you need months to find new acquisitions.

Stay in Your Price Range—Collecting should be fun. It is not enjoyable if you select a category you can't afford. Your hobby should not cause financial hardship.

Fortunately, many 1940s and 1950s collectibles are reasonably priced. Books, magazines, and many plastic, ceramic and glass items are inexpensive.

Unless you are wealthy, don't try to collect Wurlitzer jukeboxes or rare Elvis Presley autographs.

However, don't ignore the investment value of your acquisitions. Studies show that during the past decade, some antiques and collectibles increased in value faster than stocks, bonds and gold bullion.

Buy the Best You Can Afford—The investment value of your collection is a consideration. Knowledgeable dealers and collectors will tell you that high-quality items appreciate faster than ordinary examples. If you have $10 to spend, buy one item instead of 10. Its value will appreciate much more rapidly than the value of the less-expensive pieces.

Don't Buy Damaged Items—Rarity, age and condition affect investment value. Only purchase mementos that are in good condition and have not been extensively restored. The value of damaged pieces seldom increases significantly.

Upgrade Your Collection—We all change as we mature. As you become a more knowledgeable collector, you will probably decide some of your early purchases no longer interest you. Don't hesitate to sell or trade these pieces. Remember, quantity is less important than quality. A collection of 50 choice pieces is much more valuable than one with 200 ordinary or damaged pieces.

An advanced collector is always looking for something better. Your collection should grow as you do!

FINDING 1940s AND 1950s MEMORABILIA

Many collectibles from this period are stored away in attics, basements, barns, sheds, furniture warehouses and secondhand stores.

Look Close to Home—Check your house and those of your friends and relatives.

Try Secondhand Stores—Go to thrift shops and used-furniture stores. It is not unusual to find a Donald Deskey coffee table at a Salvation Army outlet.

Attend Sales and Bazaars—Yard sales and charity bazaars are excellent sources of memorabilia. If you don't find the items you are looking for, ask whether such mementos are in storage.

Many people are not aware that 1940s and 1950s memorabilia are collectible. It might not occur to them to display an old set of Russell Wright dishware.

Fortunately, most 1940s and 1950s items are easy to describe. All you need to say is that you are looking for the things people furnished their homes with at that time.

Advertise—This is often worthwhile. Type small ads describing what you are looking for and put them up in supermarkets and other places where public notices are posted. Place ads in local newspapers. Rates are often low. Run your ad several times, changing it slightly each time. Describe the items you are looking for in detail.

Visit Antique Dealers—Most dealers don't have many pieces from this period. Items they do have are usually exorbitantly priced. Secondhand stores often have similar items for more reasonable sums.

This does not mean you should never look for mementos in antique shops. Many dealers have a few decorative objects. These often include metalwares such as the Ronson lighters of the 1950s and stylish bronze figurines.

Vintage-clothing dealers may have everything from Hawaiian shirts to spike heels. These items are seldom categorized by year. You will find them among similar objects made earlier and later.

You can assemble your collection without ever visiting a dealer. Memorabilia from the 1940s and 1950s comprise one of the few collecting fields in which you and the dealers are on equal footing.

Your chances of finding things are as good as

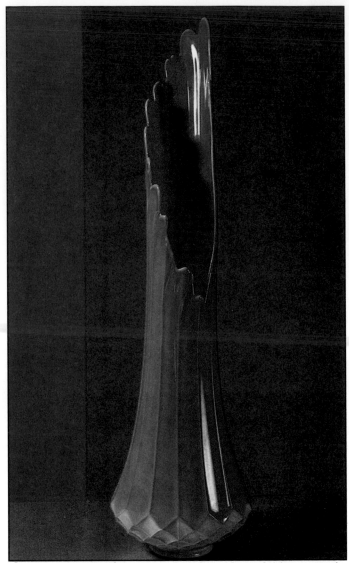

Orange was one of the most popular colors of this era, and it is used to great effect in this 3-foot-high molded vase. This piece is valued at $200 to $250. Look for glass in strong colors such as red, blue, green and yellow.

theirs. As this field becomes more popular, experienced collectors will be able to sell extra acquisitions to dealers entering the field.

Attend Auctions—You can often find memorabilia at auctions, especially those in large cities. Items from the 1940s and 1950s, especially furniture, are often sold with Art Deco and Art Nouveau pieces.

Estate auctions in smaller communities are also good sources for mementos. What the auctioneer may be offering as "used furniture" may be just what you are looking for. Items from this period may not be regarded as important enough to advertise. Attend auction viewings to see what is available.

Contacting local auctioneers is a good idea. Let them know what you are interested in. Ask them to let you know when 1940s and 1950s memorabilia are going to be sold.

Consult Other Collectors—Don't forget that other collectors can help you. You can meet them at shows or through collectors' clubs. Some clubs publish newsletters with members' names, addresses and areas of interest. Correspond with people whose interests are similar to yours. Other collectors are competitors, but they can also become good friends who can broaden your knowledge and help you find new acquisitions.

Design a Collectors' Card—This is like a business card. It includes your name, address, telephone number and interests. It might say, *Collector of 1950s Movie Memorabilia* or *Collector of Fiesta Ware*. Hand out these cards at shows, auctions and club meetings. You may get some good leads about new pieces.

BUYING AND SELLING MEMORABILIA

You will find some items in attics and basements. You will receive others as gifts. However, you will purchase the majority of your mementos. Therefore, you should know about pricing practices in the collecting world.

Supply and Demand Control Value—Prices depend on these factors. A rare piece is worth more than an item made in great quantities if the demand for both mementos is the same. However, a rare piece is worth very little if collectors are not interested in it. More readily available items may be worth much more than a rare memento if thousands of enthusiasts are collecting such items. Movie posters are a good example of this phenomenon.

Price Guides Are Helpful—These can give you approximate values for specific items. Look at the one in this book. Note auction prices and dealers' asking prices. These are very accurate when there is a well-established market for an item. Pricing is especially difficult for 1940s and 1950s memorabilia because the field is so new. Values for many items are still fluctuating. Many general price guides don't even include items from this period.

Location Affects Price—Another complicating factor is that the price of a specific piece—an Eames chair or a chrome floor lamp—will differ according to geographic location and the type of store it is in. An Eames chair would cost much more in a fancy New York City antique store than in a secondhand store in Ames, Iowa.

Condition Is Important—Most collectors will not buy a damaged item unless it is very rare and valuable. Damage can reduce the value of an object 30% to 75%.

Research Saves Money—Never sell an item without finding out what it is and what it is worth. Small details can make an enormous difference. A typical laminated wood chair by Eames is worth $250 to $300. The same chair stained red—a rare color—is worth several thousand. If you didn't know this, you might sell such a chair for $250, losing a great deal of money. Researching your acquisitions can help you avoid costly errors.

DISPLAYING YOUR COLLECTION

You can take various approaches.

Create a Period Atmosphere—Many 1940s and 1950s collectibles are used rather than displayed. Some collectors re-create a period room with appropriate wallpaper, rugs and drapes. You can do this yourself or hire an interior designer. If you want to do the work, get old copies of *Better Homes & Gardens* or *House Beautiful*. The pictures in these magazines will give you an idea what rooms looked like during this time.

Your 1940s and 1950s pieces will work best when combined with other modern furnishings. They do not usually blend well with Victorian or early-American pieces.

Use Recessed Cabinets—If you want to display objects in back-lighted cases, buy recessed cabinets. Glass shelves set in a window are a less-expensive alternative.

Display Small Objects in Groups—Try placing such items beneath a coffee table with a glass top. Or put them in shadow boxes on the wall.

Shelves and shadow boxes should be adjustable so you can rearrange your display.

Be Original—The way you display your collection should reflect your personality. Don't let someone else dictate the way you design it.

Be sure to follow several simple safety rules.

Protect Breakable Pieces—They should be fixed to a base so they cannot fall over. You can use sticky photographers' gum, clear-plastic line or two-sided tape.

Be Careful About Sunlight—If direct exposure to sunlight would damage your acquisitions, keep them out of windows or cover them with Plexiglass, which blocks ultraviolet rays.

This plastic and chrome ice bucket carries the trademark *Sav-ice* and was made by Remington Rand in the 1940s. It costs $45 to $65.

Textiles and prints are especially fragile. Wool textiles should also be protected from moths.

Be Aware of Pets—Fragile items should be out of the reach of pets.

Protect Children from Injury—Remember that children are attracted to bright, unusual-looking objects. Small items that children could put in their mouths should be kept under cover.

Shelves should be built in such a way that children cannot climb on them.

All glass display cases and shelving should be able to withstand a sharp blow or accidental tipping.

If you restore or repair your collectibles, make sure that glues, paints and paint removers are safely stored.

STORING AND SHIPPING COLLECTIBLES

You will probably have to store some of your mementos. You may occasionally have to ship items, too. Collectibles from the 1940s and 1950s vary greatly in size, shape and materials. Some are very fragile. If you follow these general rules, your acquisitions should survive storage or shipping.

Avoid Dampness—Items should not be stored in damp areas or places subject to sudden temperature changes.

Check for Insects—If you live in an area with wood worms or termites, periodically check wood objects for infestation. Fumigate storage areas.

Refold Textiles—Cloth items folded for storage should be refolded every few months. Otherwise, they might wear thin and crack along the folds.

Use Large Boxes—Your collectibles should be stored in boxes that have plenty of room. Crowding and crushing your mementos can damage them.

Protect Fragile Items—Such mementos should be wrapped in bubble pack, disposable diapers or Styrofoam fragments. They should be packed in two boxes, one inside the other. Outer boxes should be taped together and bound with cord.

CLEANING AND REPAIRING COLLECTIBLES

When cleaning items, remember one general rule—least is best.

Use Warm Water—This plus a mild detergent should be all you need. Hot water will warp or melt some plastics and will split wood veneers.

Be Careful with Abrasives—Steel wool and other abrasives should be used sparingly on metal. Never use abrasives on glass or plastics.

Test Cleaning Products—Before using rust remover or metal cleaner, apply a small amount to an inconspicuous area of the item you want to clean. Make sure the product doesn't discolor or corrode the metal.

Metals and some wood and leather can be protected from further deterioration after being thoroughly cleaned. Use commercial oils or finishing agents.

Follow the directions and don't experiment. If you make a mistake, you may damage the item irreparably.

Don't Buy Damaged Pieces—Most collectors want to buy pieces that look like new. You will find items in excellent condition if you are willing to wait. If you find a damaged item that is especially rare or valuable, have it restored professionally.

If you collect other antiques, you may find this insistence on shiny appearances surprising. After all, collectors of 19th-century furniture and accessories prize patina and signs of age.

The field of 1940s and 1950s memorabilia has different standards. If you plan to resell your acquisitions, be sure they are in prime condition and have bright, polished surfaces.

DOING RESEARCH

This field is so new that little has been written about it. You will have to do some detective work to learn about your acquisitions. This process is not as difficult as you might think. It can even be fun.

Check Manufacturers' Marks—Most objects from this period have such marks. Many marks include the city and state where the item was made. With this information you can write to the company if it is still in business. If the firm has closed, a local chamber of commerce or historical society may have data about the company.

Look for Catalogs—Many firms published advertising catalogs during this time. Try to find one featuring your mementos. Booksellers and dealers in ephemera, or paper goods, often have such catalogs.

Visit Local Libraries—You can also consult local business directories, old newspapers and census records. Your library may have these resources.

Record All Data—Write down the information you gather. It is now part of the history, or *provenance,* of the piece. This is important for you and future owners. Objects with a known history often bring higher prices than those without one.

Research can take a long time. You may spend hours without discovering much. However, this aspect of collecting can be very exciting and rewarding. Research can be like a treasure hunt. You may find important information no other collector has.

ORGANIZING YOUR COLLECTION

As the size of your collection increases, you will need to locate items and their histories quickly. The best way to do this is to set up a filing system and record book.

Use a system of numbers or letters or a combination of both. Get a small gummed label and place it on an inconspicuous part of one item. Write a number on the

Charles Eames designed this modernistic fiberglass-and-iron armchair. It was produced during the 1950s by the Herman Miller Co. of Zeeland, Michigan. It is worth $100 to $135.

COLLECTOR'S RECORD BOOK

CODE # _____

TYPE OF COLLECTIBLE _____

DATE OF PURCHASE _____

CONDITION _____

PURCHASE PRICE _____

ASSESSED VALUE _____

SOURCE OF ACQUISITION _____

_____

MANUFACTURER (IF KNOWN) _____

ORIGINAL USE _____

_____

DESCRIPTION

    SIZE _____

    COLOR _____

    SHAPE _____

    LABEL _____

    MATERIALS USED _____

    DISTINGUISHING MARKS _____

_____

RESEARCH

    PUBLICATIONS OR EXPERTS CONSULTED _____

_____

_____

    RESULTS OF RESEARCH _____

_____

_____

NOTES _____

_____

_____

Make copies of this page for your own record book.

label—for example, *45.* Now enter the same number in a large notebook or ledger.

Record whatever you know about the piece next to the number. Be sure to include where and when you got the item, the price you paid, and the history of the piece. Write down where, when and by whom it was made, the condition it was in when you bought it, and any repairs or restoration work.

If you have a photo of the item, place it in the record book.

No one can remember all the information they gather about every acquisition. After you compile your record book, you will be able to obtain any information you need quickly and easily. If you have a computer, consider storing this data in your machine. It will make record-keeping easier as your collection becomes larger.

INSURANCE AND SECURITY

Collectors must think about security. You might decide to install special locks or gates, an electronic security system, or a guard dog. What you do depends on the value of your collection, where you live and how much you want to spend.

The best security system is a group of concerned neighbors. Join or start a Neighborhood Watch program. Let your neighbors know you will watch their property and ask them to watch yours.

Ask your police department for tips on home security. Officers can also label your items so they can be easily identified if they are stolen.

Theft is only one problem. Fire, earthquakes, floods, hurricanes and tornadoes can devastate your home and your collection.

Many enthusiasts insure their possessions. If you decide to do this, remember that most companies want an *appraisal,* or statement of value. This requires an expert knowledgeable in the field. Companies usually want a photograph of each important piece, too.

This can be expensive. However, it is money well-spent if it protects your investment.

PHOTOGRAPHING YOUR COLLECTION

One way you can cut costs is by doing your own photography. Use a 35mm camera. Instant-picture cameras are not recommended because the photos are usually not detailed enough.

Use white paper or cloth as a background. You can shoot indoors with a flash, but you get better results outside on a sunny day.

Photograph each piece separately. Follow the camera directions and take your time. You will be surprised at the results. In three or four hours you can take 15 to 20 shots. You would have to pay a professional several hundred dollars to take the same number of pictures.

Photographs are helpful for insurance purposes.

They also provide a valuable record of your collection. If you have a large group of similar objects, taking your record book and photos on buying trips will prevent you from purchasing duplicates.

Some of the suggestions about building and caring for your collection may seem like a great deal of work. However, all these steps are part of a fascinating process. They help you learn about the things you love and how to safeguard them. In a very real sense, all collectors are historians and guardians of our national cultural heritage. You may not work in a museum, but in a way you own one!

Collectors pay high prices for figural cookie jars. This Little Red Riding Hood was produced in the 1940s by the A. E. Hull Pottery Co. of Crooksville, Ohio. It is valued at $45 to $65.

Price Guide

Whatever 1940s and 1950s memorabilia you decide to collect, you should know about prevailing prices. Some items are easier to price than others. This guide will give you approximate values.

Remember that a price guide is *only* a guide. It provides general information. Prices in this field are not fixed. They fluctuate frequently.

SUPPLY AND DEMAND

The most important factor in determining price is supply and demand. No matter how old or rare something is, it is not worth much unless there is a demand for it. You may think one of your mementos is a wonderful collectible. However, if no one else wants it, the item has little monetary value.

The demand for items made during the 1940s and 1950s is increasing. Many types of items are bought and sold fairly frequently.

Collectors and dealers usually base their prices on the amount they have paid in the past. This amount is the *base price*. Sellers usually add a 15% to 25% profit margin to the base price. Dealers also include another 5% to 10% for *overhead,* or business costs. Overhead includes shop rental, utility bills and advertising. The final price—including base price, profit margin and overhead—is called the *asking price*.

Remember that collectibles are not like stereos or automobiles. When dealers or collectors sell an item, they can't simply call the factory and order an identical replacement at the price they paid previously. When they look for another item, they will have to consult other dealers and collectors. They may find the price has increased significantly since the last time they purchased a similar item. This is one reason prices in this field vary so much.

This book lists a range of prices for each item to compensate for fluctuations. If the price guide says an item costs $55 to $80, these figures represent the highest and lowest amounts you could expect to pay.

POINTS TO REMEMBER

No book can cover every object in such a large field. This price guide lists key items in each category. Use these prices to help determine the values of comparable pieces. Keep several guidelines in mind.

Damaged Items Are Worth Less—Prices listed in this book are for collectibles in good, average condition with normal wear. Damaged or restored items are worth 30% to 75% less. If an item is extensively damaged or has many missing parts, don't buy it. For example, never purchase a table with a top that has been replaced, or a piece of pottery that has been broken and glued together.

Check Acquisitions Carefully—Most dealers and collectors are honest. They will tell you what has been done to a piece if they know. However, some sellers are unscrupulous. You must protect yourself.

Don't Pay Too Much—If the asking price is well above the one listed in this guide, it is too high.

Let your experience guide you, too. Paying $100 for a chrome tea set that lists for $65 will encourage the seller to charge an even higher price for the next set. It will also make it difficult for you to break even if you decide to sell the piece in the near future.

High prices hurt all collectors. They are also unnecessary. Duplicates of most 1940s and 1950s items can usually be found fairly quickly.

Iron-wire furniture was one of the greatest design innovations of the 1950s.
This wire and leather stool costs $75 to $95. The wire ashtray stand with glass
ashtray is worth $35 to $45.

Small stacking tables or stools in lacquered hardwood cost $65 to $150. They were made in the early 1950s.

This pair of tubular-steel and plastic side chairs was produced in the late 1940s. Their slim lines and appealing colors ensure their continuing popularity with collectors. These pieces cost $85 to $135 each.

The Thonet firm of Austria has made chairs since the 19th century. This lacquered bentwood armchair was produced for the American market during the 1940s and early 1950s. It is valued at $200 to $400.

This modern free-form desk of lacquered pine was designed by Paul Frankl. Although very simple in construction, this piece is worth $500 to $750. It was manufactured in the 1940s.

These double cabinets were included with bedroom sets. This piece dates from the 1940s or early 1950s and was made in the Midwest. It costs $250 to $400.

George Nelson created this slat bench, which could also be used as a table or cabinet base. It was made during the 1950s, and is worth $750 to $1,200.

This Danish Modern sideboard is molded plywood. It was made from 1940 until 1950 and is worth $225 to $400.

This set of frosted tumblers has its own wood and iron-wire carrying rack. It dates from the 1950s. The complete set is worth $40 to $55. Individual glasses cost $1 to $2.

Known as *grain ware* because of its grainy surface, these plastic serving dishes were designed to resemble carved ebony. Made during the 1940s and 1950s, these pieces are attracting collectors' attention. Prices are $5 to $8 for the small round serving bowls and $15 to $20 for the large platter.

Hand-blown glass objects from Venice were in great demand during the postwar period. The striped bowl costs $125 to $175; the bottle, $100 to $150; the handkerchief vase, $300 to $450. These items were made between 1945 and 1960.

The 1950s produced some odd designs that occasionally reflected a 1940s influence. This brightly colored combination sugar bowl/salt/pepper shaker reminds one of a Carmen Miranda hat. It is worth $2 to $5.

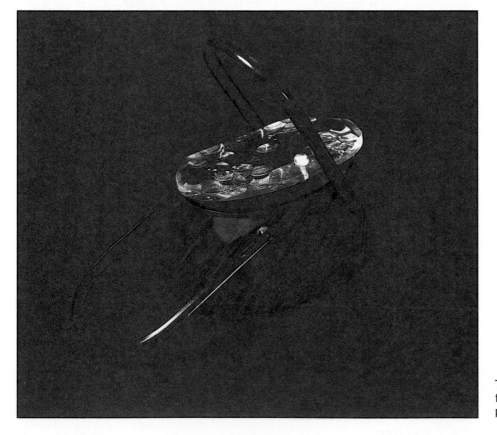

This double-handled purse from the 1950s is mock tortoise-shell plastic. It is worth $25 to $40.

The pink flamingo, one of the most popular symbols of the 1950s, dominates these Japanese plastic and chrome serving trays. Made between 1955 and 1960, these pieces are an adaptation of an ancient Japanese design. Prices are $5 to $10 for the small tray, $8 to $15 for the large one.

Made in Italy during the 1950s for export to the United States, these ceramic animals are typical of the whimsical figures popular with collectors today. The dog is worth $50 to $75. The bird costs $65 to $95.

Souvenir plates such as these have always had their
enthusiasts. All are marked *Florida.* The one with the
flamingo costs $35 to $45. The other two are worth $25 to
$35 each.

Russell Wright tableware was made in these five colors.
Cups and saucers are $25 to $35; plates are $15 to $20;
the handled sugar bowl is $25 to $35; the pitcher is $45 to
$60.

During the 1940s and 1950s, "naturalistic" pottery such as this sugar bowl with an ear-of-corn motif was popular. Made by Shawnee Pottery of Zanesville, Ohio, it is priced at $10 to $14.

Look for decorator china. These pieces were designed by Eva Zeisel for the Hall China Co. of East Liverpool, Ohio. They are worth $2 to $10 each. A complete 50-piece set for eight costs $250 to $350.

Fiesta Ware plates come in a large variety of pieces. These
examples range from 6-inch dessert plates to 15-inch
chop plates, and are valued at $2 to $12 each.

Look for radios in spectacular colors. These plastic
examples include a black-and-white check G.E. Youth
Electronics worth $150 to $200, and a red Emerson worth
$225 to $350. Both date from the 1950s.

Bakelite plastic bracelets are fashionable today. Priced
reasonably at $5 to $20, these pieces are interesting and
durable.

These rhinestone and metal bracelets date from the 1950s. Expansion types cost $65 to $100. Other examples cost $45 to $65. Condition is important. Make sure no stones are missing.

Just what the well-dressed collector wants! The cloth hat is a bargain at $10 to $20. The rhinestone necklace costs $50 to $65. The plaster mannequin is $85 to $145.

Simple rayon dresses from the 1940s are being worn by collectors. This dress, priced at $45 to $55, has the bright colors popular at that time.

Charm bracelets were a major fad from 1945 to 1960. This spectacular example in gold costs $1,200 to $1,550. Less-expensive examples in silver or pot metal sell for $75 to $350.

Fur-trimmed jackets are fun. They are also a good investment. Most collectors wear these items. This garment is an excellent buy at $65 to $85. It was made between 1945 and 1955.

This taffeta jacket, fully lined and expertly tailored, is as
fashionable right now as it was in the 1940s. Though the
jacket is high-style dressing, it is a super buy at $15 to $25.

Davy Crockett memorabilia were very popular during the 1950s. This coonskin cap is a bargain at $15 to $20.
When collecting memorabilia of such fictional characters as Davy Crockett, Red Rider and the Lone Ranger,
remember that most items were made in great quantities. Don't assume that an example is unique.

Tin canister sets such as this are interesting and practical.
Made about 1950, this set is worth $30 to $45. Individual
tins cost $5 to $7.

These notepad holders, made from 1945 to 1955, are
popular collectibles. Left to right: Painted wood, $20 to
$30; plaster, $35 to $50; molded plastic, $30 to $45.

These pillows have the geometric shapes typical of the 1950s. They are worth $25 to $35 each.

The parrot was a popular symbol during the postwar years. These carved, painted wood examples were wall decorations. The small piece costs $18 to $26. The large one is $27 to $38.

Chrome tableware and utensils are becoming more valuable. These items were made during the 1950s. The waffle irons are worth $10 to $20 each. The toaster costs $20 to $30. Have an electrician check your purchases before you use them. Buy utensils in working condition.

Metalware can be extremely attractive. Left to right: Enameled copper centerpiece, $85 to $145; ball-shaped chrome and plastic ashtray, $55 to $75; anodized copper bowl, $75 to $125. All were made in the 1950s.

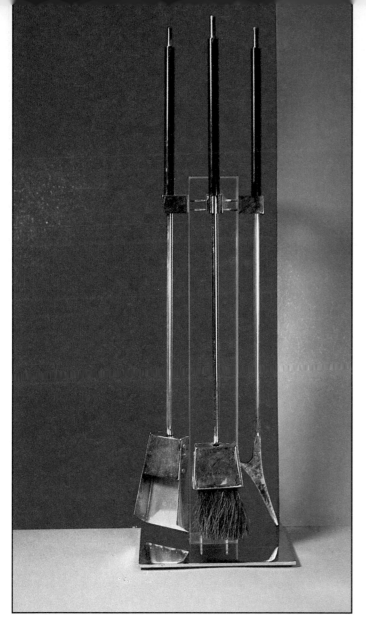

These sleek stainless-steel and lucite fireplace tools date from the 1950s and are worth $250 to $350.

Unusual forms such as the oval and amoeba were characteristic of the 1950s. The footed pewter nut dish costs $45 to $60. The other item is worth $35 to $55.

Bibliography

This recommended list of books can help when you research collectibles from the 1940s and 1950s. Some of these books may be out of print and probably won't be readily available at bookstores. Others are privately printed or published by small, regional publishers. These too may be difficult to find. Therefore, you should supplement this list with books available from local libraries or used bookstores.

Allen, Frederick C. *Only Yesterday.* New York, NY: Harper & Row, 1957.

Archer, Margaret and Douglas. *Imperial Glass.* Paducah, KY: Collectors Books, 1978.

Barnicost, John. *A Concise History of Posters.* New York, NY: Harry Abrams, 1976.

Botts, Rick. *1983 Jukebox Collectors' Dictionary.* Privately printed, 1983.

Brown, Sheldon. *Official Price Guide to Radio, TV and Movie Memorabilia.* Orlando, FL: The House of Collectibles, 1985.

Buxton, Virginia. *Roseville Pottery for Love or Money.* Nashville, TN: Tymbre Hill Publishing Co., 1977.

Corbin, Patricia. *All About Wicker.* New York, NY: EP Dutton, 1978.

Cosentino, Geraldine, and Stewart, Regina. *Kitchenware.* New York, NY: Western Publishin Company, 1976.

Cranor, Rosalind. *Elvis Collectibles.* Paducah, KY: Collectors Books, 1983.

Cunningham, Jo. *The Collectors' Encyclopedia of American Dinnerware.* Paducah, KY: Collectors Books, 1982.

Dempsey, Jimmy. *Encyclopedia and Price Guide of Radio Premiums.* Privately printed, 1982.

Florence, Gene. *A Pocket Guide to Depression Glass.* Paducah, KY: Collectors Books, 1980.

Grief, Martin. *Depression Modern: The Thirties Style in America.* New York, NY: Universe Books, 1975.

Hammond, Dorothy. *Confusing Collectibles: A Guide to the Identification of Contemporary Objects.* Des Moines, IA: Hollow Homestead Book Company, 1978.

Hillier, Bevis. *The World of Art Deco.* New York, NY: E.P. Dutton, 1981.

Hudgeons, Thomas E. III, ed. *Official Price Guide to Paper Collectibles.* Orlando, FL: House of Collectibles, 1983.

Huxford, Sharon and Robert. *The Collector's Encyclopedia of Fiesta.* Paducah, KY: Collectors Books, 1978.

Kaplan, Arthur. *Official 1982 Price Guide to Antique Jewelry.* Orlando, FL: House of Collectibles, 1981.

Kerr, Ann. *Russel Wright and His Dinnerware: A Descriptive Price Guide.* Privately printed, 1979.

Ketchum, William C. Jr. *The Catalog of American Collectibles.* New York, NY: Gallery, 1979.

McMahon, Morgan E. *Vintage Radio* (2 volumes). Palos Verdes, CA: Vintage Radio, Inc., 1973.

Morrow, Lynn. *Black Collectibles.* Privately printed, 1976.

Page, Marion. *Furniture Designed by Architects.* New York, NY: Whitney Library of Design, Watson Guptill Publications, 1980.

Ray, Marcia. *An Encyclopedia of Pottery and Porcelain.* Hanover, PA: Everybody's Press, 1976.

Sieloff, Julie. *Collectibles of Occupied Japan.* Des Moines, IA: Wallace-Homestead Book Co., 1977.

Weatherman, Hazel Marie. *Colored Glassware of the Depression Era* (2 volumes). Springfield, MO: privately printed, 1970, 1974.

Zemel, Evelyn. *American Glass Animals from A to Z.* North Miami, FL: privately printed, 1978.

Index